STATEMENT

" Cybersecurity is the heart of a proper functioning of our new society, for its survival and for its relationship with Nations. The mastery of cyberspace and intelligence tools should be the deterrent weapon in terms of national security policy:

Therefore, Electronic warfare, and cyber warfare should precede that of soldiers' boots".

Charles K. KOKO

NATIONAL
SECURITY BOX

Hacking & Cyberattacks Against Critical Infrastructures - The Challenge of Cyberwar at Europe Doorsteps & United Kingdom.

Charles K KOKO
Cyber Security

PREFACE

National Security Box is a new and exciting book that goes deep into the Science of Cyber Security, the author brings you into a new world in which our new society has no trust. This loss of trust, reshuffling cards for the control of perimeters that have long been associated with buffer territories. It is another moment of reconquests, but this time, new actors clearly appear: the Cybersecurity.

The world is experiencing difficult moments of geopolitical turbulence with several crises around. Nations conquer new spaces, sometimes to the detriment of other peoples, and on the other hand, peoples who have long felt oppressed by their governments, aspire to more sovereignty and claim it on a simple ethnic, linguistic, and religious basis. The Covid 19 health crisis, and the Ukrainian war are reviving tensions that have long been forgotten, and NATO seen as an instrument of influence of the United States, keeps expanding and annoys Russia which itself has ambitions to reconstitute a lost empire. France looks with more greed on an African continent out of breath particularly those French speaking countries which in turn look towards Russia leading to adversity between France and Russia and which translates on Ukrainian soil through means of cyberattacks and intelligence.

All these conflicts, even invisible exist, and stir up tensions between actors. The proxy warfare is real and cybersecurity is at the center of it: "All the sauces are gathered" for a physical confrontation between States as the cyberwar has already started. Cyberattacks perpetrated by NATO and Russia against each other's infrastructures are decried and denounced by either party that lead them. This legalized hypocrisy at the top level of States, is legitimized by the obsession to emerge victorious from the war of communication by using public media means. In view of all this, implementing a cybersecurity document at this particular time where the world is holding its breath, is essential for our communities and more importantly for those in charge of protecting our infrastructures, vital for our survival.

CONTENTS

- ➤ Confidentiality Attacks
- ➤ Advanced Persistent Attacks (APT)
- ➤ Backdoors.
- ➤ File transfer protocol (FTP).
- ➤ FTP Protocol Vulnerabilities (FTP Bounce Attack)
- ➤ Passive Aggressive Attacks
- ➤ Stuxnet Attacks
- ➤ Flame or Duqu Attacks
- ➤ DNA Attacks
- ➤ Social Engineering Attacks (Common Social Engineering Attacks)
- ➤ Spear Phishing
- ➤ Baiting Techniques
- ➤ Data Leakage
- ➤ The Imminent And Non-Negligible Attacks.
- ➤ Electromagnetic Pulsed: Targeted Attack.
- ➤ Attaxks Aimed to Alter Information & Process (Integrity Attacks)
- ➤ DoS Attacks
- ➤ Access Attacks
- ➤ Password Attacks
- ➤ Trust Exploitation Attacks
- ➤ Man In-The Middle Attack
- ➤ Recognition Attacks
- ➤ Recon-type Attacks
- ➤ Malware Attacks
- ➤ Other Attacks
- ➤ Attack by DHCP
- ➤ ARP Poisoning Attack
- ➤ Spoofing Attacks
- ➤ Sniffing Attacks
- ➤ Application Layer Attack
- ➤ Flooding Attack and Rouge Devices
- ➤ Ransomware
- ➤ Identification Vulnerability
- ➤ Vulnerability Assessment (Pen-Testing)
- ➤ System Protection
- ➤ Main Applications of Artificial Intelligence in Cyber Security

Chapter 3

- ➤ Security Of SCADA Within Critical Infrastructure
- ➤ Application control and identity support
- ➤ Firewall
- ➤ Intrusion prevention
- ➤ Antivirus
- ➤ Emulation threats
- ➤ Business Plan
- ➤ 5-Step Method
- ➤ Recovery Plan
- ➤ Resilience
- ➤ Performance Values
- ➤ Breakdown of the Resilience Indicator
- ➤ Ethical Considerations
- ➤ Literature Review
- ➤ Methodology
- ➤ Findings
- ➤ Results
- ➤ Sizes of Companies
- ➤ Survey Results
- ➤ Respondents who have experienced cyberattack
- ➤ Total of Respondents

Chapter 4

- ➤ Data Analysis
- ➤ Discussion
- ➤ Analysing Most Active SCADA Systems:
- ➤ Conclusions
- ➤ Recommendations
- ➤ Glossary
- ➤ References
- ➤ Bibliography
- ➤ Appendix A: Project Plan

FIGURES

TABLES

ACKNOWLEDGMENTS

The realization of this book was possible thanks to the help of several people to whom I would like to express my gratitude.

A big thank you to my daughters Claysha and Shaneika Koko and my son Aroence Koko for their love, their advice as well as their unconditional support, both moral and social, which allowed me to realize the researches that I wanted and therefore this book.

I would also like to express my gratitude to Grace Citte, Naveck and Kamissa for their invaluable support and trust.

I especially wish to thank my parents Pauline and Pierre who have not been fortunate enough to be with us today for their moral and financial support during all the time of my youth and to whom I dedicate this book.

Finally, Since the investigative part of this book was carried out during my thesis in Cyber Security, I would like to thank all the employees of Buckinghamshire New University through which institution, I obtained an agreement that I presented to IT professionals or/and Risk Management Teams from different organizations in charge of vital infrastructures I visited, to obtain interviews from them, thus allowing me to convince and reassure them about the legitimacy of my project. For this, I express my gratitude to Dr Rafid Alkhannak, Justin Luker, Prof. Philip Wood, Dr Carlo Lusuardi and Prof. Richard Jones without whom this agreement would not have been possible.

ABSTRACT

This book will help develop an assessment of the use of cybersecurity tools and techniques to avoid and counter a cyber-attack on critical infrastructure in the context of cyber warfare between countries or between a country and a group of aggressors or against terrorists with or without any political motivation.

This is part of the efforts of several months of library research, university recommendation tools, books and survey, as well as the support of experts. The purpose of this paper is to develop a new vision of sustainable techniques to mitigate risks and detect vulnerabilities long before the attack occurs. It aims to build a body of knowledge around security tools used to protect these infrastructures, knowledge of the analysis of how the system works and what will need to be done to protect them against a potential cyberattack.

This book seeks to assess the state of safety of critical infrastructures in Europe and the UK and also to determine how hackers are performing in the new approach of utilising new technologies to perform an attack against critical infrastructures. Analytical techniques will also be used to determine the attackers' state of mind and to test their ability to harm and better cope with this challenge; their motivation, purpose or ultimate goal. Do they work for themselves or are they supported by States. Are they inside Europe, where are they located, and how do they operate? This is a project that takes a closer look at the physical state of critical infrastructure at the gateway of Europe and in the United Kingdom, and identifies what aspects of infrastructure improvement and maintenance can contribute to more sustainable security for States and more reliability for users, who are usually civilian populations.

The crucial importance of the research-based in this book is indisputable in that, it will analyze and provide first-hand insight into the state and conditions of operation of all critical infrastructures, whether private or government-owned, in the United Kingdom and in Europe. The method will consist of collecting data from IT professionals and decision-makers to analyze them and make recommendations.

INTRODUCTION

National security is a fluid concept that countries translate into various sub-elements and approaches based on several factors and perceptions rooted in their history, their geographic location or their geopolitical context. In most cases, it encompasses principles, policies, procedures and functions which aim to guarantee independence, the sovereignty and integrity of a State and the rights of its citizens. European countries expressly include the protection of critical infrastructure among their national security priorities. Establishing a close link between the protection of critical infrastructure and national security goals can help provide support for strengthened policy for the further development of specific strategies for the protection of critical infrastructures and to encourage their implementation.

Everything, including the critical national infrastructures (CNI), is becoming increasingly connected, resulting in increased vulnerability and greater exposure to real physical risk (House of Lords and House of Commons, 2018). Hydraulic dams, communication infrastructures, production pipelines, distribution of water, traffic lights, and nuclear reactors include elements, systems and networks that are vulnerable to attacks, and the Internet of Things (IoT) OR/AND the Bring Your Own Device (BYOD) connected to them; could cripple the economy, public health and safety and can jeopardize national security in the event of an attack.

Numerous industrial infrastructures, chemical factories, refineries and power plants manage their installations thanks to electronic systems, Supervisory Control And Data Acquisition (SCADA) (Pillai *et al.*, 2012), which regulate the different flows by sending orders to PLCs (Programmable Logic Controllers).

PLCs are central to the functioning of the SCADA system but are subject to cyberattacks (Wang *et al.*, 2018) commonly referred to as Cyber-Physical Attacks, subject of a sustained investigation in this book. What would happen if PLCs are victims of such attacks? The research work that initialed this book consisted in providing an answer to this question by analyzing the functioning of SCADA Systems; their advantages and flaws. The first great advantage of this book is that it helps in determining or/and understanding the motivations of those who endanger the survival of a State by attacking its vital infrastructures essential to the proper functioning of our new society with more and more sophisticated means, and also to understand the stakes of such relentlessness. Who finances them and for what purpose do they attack critical infrastructures? Why are they almost never worried? Who protects them? Or how do they protect themselves? More importantly, how do they operate. There is no commonly accepted definition of the term "critical infrastructure", nor is there unanimous recognition of critical areas. Definitions vary depending on the context, including the national context, in which the expression is used (Ritter, Weber, 2004). However, does the analysis of existing definitions allow us to grasp what characterizes a critical infrastructure? To what extent does the fact that the criticality of certain sectors is discussed shed light on the political nature of the question of critical infrastructures? European countries and the UK with a CNI protection strategy each have their own definition. Even if they all agree to define them as infrastructures whose malfunction could cause significant damage to a country, its population and its economy. The few nuances that exist are particularly so in the sense of the adjective "critical" as shown in the table 1.

Examples of definitions of critical infrastructure

Table 1: European countries' definitions of critical infrastructure (Ceps Task Force Report, 2010)

Countries	Definitions
EU	Critical infrastructures are physical installations, the systems or elements of these systems are essential to the maintenance of the vital functions of society, health, security, and of the economic and social well-being of the population and whose shutdown or destruction could have significant consequences for a country due to the inability to maintain these functions. They are located in EU member countries whose termination in one country could have significant consequences in at least two EU countries. The significance of the consequences should be assessed using cross-sectoral criteria, taking into account the effects of interdependencies between sectors on other types of infrastructure (Directive, 2008)
UK	National critical infrastructures are infrastructures for which the continuity of activity is so important for the proper functioning of the nation that its loss, interruption or degradation could have consequences in terms of loss of life, economy or other serious social consequences for the community and is a major problem for the government **(ministry of interior)**

Netherlands	The Dutch approach does not give a specific definition of the term. On the other hand, it distinguishes products and services vital for the nation from those simply very important. A product or service is considered vital if it provides an essential contribution to society to maintain a minimum level of: quality, maintaining national and international legal order, public safety, economic activity, health public, environmental and ecological quality, or if the loss or malfunction of these products or services affects citizens and the governmental administration on a national scale (**National Coordination Centre 2004**).
France	A sector of activity of vital importance is made up of activities contributing to the same objective, which: 1. relate to the production and distribution of essential goods or services. a) The satisfaction of essential needs for the life of the populations or: b) The exercise of State authority, c) The functioning of the economy d) Maintaining the defence potential e) To the security of the nation (site CGDN)
Germany	Critical infrastructures are organizations and establishments which are of particular importance for the public sector and whose defect or disruption would cause lasting shortages of supplies, considerable dysfunctions in public security and other dramatic consequences (BundesMinisterium des Innem 2005)

If the motivations behind cyberattacks are extremely variable, their impact is often paralyzing for businesses, their customers or even society. Indeed, there have been recent attacks on vital public infrastructure such as hospitals; according to Postnote (2017), the war of intrusion is real, as of May 2017, many hospitals in the United Kingdom had to cancel certain medical procedures and send ambulances to other facilities following a cyberattack on NHS (National Health Service) known as WannaCry cyberattack; which is an Intrusion often sometimes led by States or by their financial contribution leading to a total paralysis of the entire system of information, data transfer, and communication.

In this context of growing threats, the security of critical infrastructures is a critical issue within Europe and in the UK (POSTnote, 2017), and this paper is intended to help leaders, regardless of the size of their organization, to interact with their risk management teams to develop Cyber Risk Management practices to eliminate or mitigate risks and be ready to quickly recover from the attack and ensuring the continuity of their businesses.

Hence, this book aims at exposing the stakes, the nature and the specificities of the cyber risk, to evoke the difficulties of its management in the company and open some lines of reflection to overcome the obstacles and develop transversal support.

CHAPTER I

- ❖ Rationality
- ❖ Research Aim
- ❖ Research Objectives
- ❖ Critical Infrastructure Risk Context
- ❖ Typology of Attackers
- ❖ Typology of Threats
- ❖ Typology of Risks
- ❖ Design & Security Platform

RATIONALITY

The rationality of this research should help all IT professionals to assimilate concepts that will allow them to overcome the difficulties related to the cyberattack that they encounter or that they will encounter throughout their careers. They will be able to offer immediate solutions to eradicate or mitigate risks and anticipate an attack by proposing a preventive response to the problem.

Being aware of all the tools proposed in this book, not only will be an asset in their way of managing the different risks linked to a cyberattack but also to be able to propose their document capable of doing the same work as that proposed in this book. They would thus discover their hidden ability which is that of defining with clarity and professionalism, policies' documentation to be implemented in the case of a cyberattack they may face. This paper will serve as a guideline in the fight against this scourge and in the protection of the critical infrastructure for which IT professionals are responsible. However, some of them have little knowledge of the effort and work that goes into implementing such a document, or even how such a "complexity" can be achieved with a minimum of knowledge. Defense tools proposed in this paper are an excellent way to establish a connection between the professionals who will become aware of this work and the objective of the project, because they will be able to experience their learning in a more "tangible" way. In addition, this book focused mainly on the identification of critical infrastructures according to the EU definition and their protection against risks run from prevention to mitigation and from risk management to resilience.

Offering tools for the security of CIs as a guideline by an IT professional within his company is by no means easy: apart from implementing such policies and tools, there are employees' education and policy updates. Employees must be taught in a way that they understand the whole strategy around the policy implemented and their objective to avoid abusively using or not using them at all. This will avoid substantive errors which may result in either a partial erasure of the policies without even realizing it or making a copy of them on any paper reachable by others. Hence the importance of implementing access authorization policies so that these policies are used and appreciated to their maximum potential. If this is done correctly, the document proposed by the professionals has everything to succeed and prove their qualities as IT leaders. It should also be noted that employees who find a document that is easy to use will be more efficient and more likely to spot flaws in the system and even suggest improvements. These employees may in turn be able to implement a proper document as they progress in their careers.

RESEARCH AIM

This research work made it possible to apply the reflection on the identification of critical infrastructures (CIs) to the case of European CIs. It also provided a privileged place for observers to verify the hypothesis of political criticality proposed by this work through how the EU debates what constitutes a critical infrastructure and a criticality threshold relating to the consequences for the population, economy, and, socio-political effects.

This constituted both the identification of the CIs and the understanding of the functioning of the EU, of its relations with the member states, in the face of the protection to be provided to their CIs. This research aims to provide new tools for the professionals of the operating Systems, network operators, and experts in cyber security to be both able to detect the flaws of the systems they use before the cyber activists exploit them to lead a coordinated attack, but also and above all to give them new ways to contain an imminent attack.

The use of these tools will help assess the compliance of defense and attack policies in real-time to protect critical infrastructures, and avoid having to postpone an incident with dramatic consequences. More importantly, these tools will help targeted industrial sites, the potential for a cyberattack to update their systems by performing regular software updates so that they do not end up with obsolete and therefore vulnerable solutions. In addition, full and continuous visibility of what is happening on their networks in real-time will be highlighted on both the IT hardware and operating technologies at the operational level, to enable much more effective and efficient protection of the systems; the detection of an anomaly or an unusual activity as soon as it occurs is thus facilitated.

OBJECTIVES
RESEARCH

The first objective of this research is conceptual, insofar as the question of critical infrastructure (CI) has, a priori, been little addressed in cybersecurity: this is explained on the one hand, because of the recent character of the problem, on the other hand, due to the disciplinary scattering which characterizes the approaches on CIs.

However, within all of the disciplines concerned (political science, economics, etc.), even late, it is above all the engineering sciences which have taken hold of the problem. It is therefore a question of returning to the concept of critical infrastructure, emphasizing its technological and spatial dimension; thus being in line with the work on the analysis of risks and vulnerability.

The second objective is methodological: it is to show how important it is to base the identification of critical infrastructure on a cyber security approach and that this approach responds to the difficulties encountered by current approaches. The latter is often limited to the "technical" dimension of the infrastructure and is very often sectoral (separate analysis of the transport, energy, medical infrastructure or water sector). By adopting a territorial point of view, it first becomes possible to go beyond the sectoral division to focus instead on the services necessary for the functioning of this territory. This then makes it possible to consider infrastructure systems in their socio-technical dimensions, which is fundamental to understanding why they are considered "critical".

The third and final objective is operational and functional: this research work constitutes an opportunity to develop a methodology for identifying CIs (essential networks), which constitutes support for decision' help for the various actors concerned by the question. Support is designed as a "toolbox", capable of adapting to different scales of analysis and decisions to overcome the deficiency in terms of security and protection of these infrastructures, deemed critical.

CRITICAL
INFRASTRUCTURES
RISKS CONTEXT

The rhythm with which everything has become inextricably interconnected has exposed the entire computer system to a set of unprecedented threats and vulnerabilities (Interpol 2018). This instability of the new society has led to mistrust between citizens and between states, leading to the famous "Uncle Sam is watching you", a theory of the conspiracy invented by the US (Maret 2016), which increased with the Bush Administration era.

Asymmetric conflicts and modes of action, including terrorist actions that characterize them have reinforced and changed the potential threats to critical infrastructures and after the attacks of September 11, 2001, the United States, the EU and its Member States gradually redesigned their approach to critical infrastructure protection. The cyberattack against the Ukrainian network in the winter of 2015 in the context of conflict with Russia has also revived the interest in these infrastructures.

It is in this context that the united nations security council has called on member States to develop "risk reduction strategies" posed by terrorist attacks against critical infrastructures and to strengthen their cooperation to counter such attacks. With resolution 2341 (2017), the Council unanimously adopted its first-ever text on the subject, during a debate that saw several senior UN officials and around fifty delegations insist on the vulnerability of critical infrastructures, tragically recalled by the attacks perpetrated at Brussels and Istanbul airports in 2016; and by this resolution, the Council calls on the Member States to take "preparatory measures" to effectively respond to attacks against such infrastructure and to affirm the criminal responsibility of those responsible for the attack. And about the cooperation component, States agreed to participate "actively" in the "prevention, protection, mitigation, preparedness, investigation, response and recovery" efforts related to potential attacks.

However, after the Stuxnet (Fruhlinger, 2017) affair exposed the flaws of the industrial systems, the risks and threats to them become a major concern for operators, as well as for States and even businesses. If the apprehension of security is mainly through good practices, it is also necessary to identify the vulnerabilities which the business has to face, make it possible to identify the areas particularly threatened within the organization and deduce the generalized basic protection recommendations. Cyber attackers have various profiles, including hacker isolated, unhappy employees, organized networks, and intelligence units. They have a multitude of motivations, such as computer challenge, data theft for profit, hacker activism, espionage for economic or industrial, and for military purposes; dependence of the army on submarine cables in the theater of operations, through the concept of network-centric warfare has proven that the permanence and availability of the submarine network are therefore security and defines issues for a nation. Many vulnerabilities weigh on the network and make this system a security priority.

Typology of attackers

Table 2: Typology of the attackers (Own research, 2019-2020)

Attackers	Characteristics	Objectives
1	PLAYFUL: Idle teenager	Sabotage
2	POLITICS: Hacktivists, Cyber-patriots, Cyber-terrorists	Spying, Massive fraud, Act-Prop, Invasion
3	LUCRATIVES: Cybergangs, Cybermercenarians, Officines	Spying, Sabotage, Invasion
4	MILITARY: Specialized Units	Invasion, Act-Prop, Spying, Saturation
5	TECHNIQUE: Hacker	Massive fraud, Saturation
6	PATHOS: Disgruntled Employee	Saturation, deleting

Cyber-attacks can originate from:

- inside the company operating the industrial system (internal threats due to inappropriate behaviour of staff when using news technologies or malice and because of a lack of governance increased, for example, by the admission and management of BYOD and WI-FI connections).
- outside the company: hacktivism, Advanced Persistent Threats (APT).

Risk typology

Table 3: Typology of risks (Own research, 2019-2020)

Risks	Specificity of industrial systems
Loss of data and service interruptions	Notwithstanding the existence of backups and procedures for restoring lost data, such a risk would have serious consequences for the industrial system ranging from irreparable damage to equipment to loss of human life.
Response time, downtime and delays	The essence of industrial systems that is real-time operation, no significant delay or other downtime is tolerated.
Equipment restart and hot backup	Dangerous consequences up to and including damage to property and people.
Lack of data encryption	Transmission of unencrypted data between the various components and to the outside of the industrial system.
Non-regular penetration tests	Non-regular penetration tests are not part of corporate culture. They are however necessary and the greatest care must be given to them in order to

	guarantee the continuity of activity.
Lack of security audits	They weren't considered necessary in the past
The lifetime of the equipment making up the system	There is no replacement or upgrade of equipment, they are designed for very long lifespans
The vulnerability of the networks and equipment to which the system is connected	The use of vulnerable remote connections and / or platforms with known vulnerabilities

The requirement for a basic protection concept arises between other legal provisions and standards generally admitted, but also, in general, business principles admitted to forward risk management and strategic planning geared to success and continuity – by example as part of said business continuity plan (BCP)

Some manufacturers are reluctant to adopt the latest generation of SCADA systems, mistakenly believing that they are vulnerable to cybercrime attacks. Some of them also believe that SCADA networks that are physically secure and disconnected from the Internet are sufficiently secure. In reality, as SCADA systems can be used for monitoring and controlling strategic processes like water distribution, traffic light management, electricity distribution, gas transport, submarine cables etc., it is good logical to ask the question about possible hacks of the system and their consequences.

There are two major threats when it comes to SCADA systems. The first is unauthorized access to software, intentionally made by humans or inadvertent changes, viral infections and any other problem that could affect the control machine. The second threat is related to packet access to network segments hosting SCADA systems. In many cases, providers provide little security to the packet control protocol. So anyone who sends packets to the system could control it. However, it is very easy to secure the system. For example, users can use VPN security to ensure sufficient protection. SCADA providers can also avoid these risks by setting up industrial firewalls specifically dedicated to SCADA networks based on TCP / IP. In addition, whitelist solutions can be implemented and are capable of preventing unauthorized changes to applications.

The cyber risk analysis particularly illustrates the need for a dialogue at the highest level of the company between the security directorates, the information system security managers and the risk management team. The need for "cross-cooperation" responds to the multiplicity of issues. Cyber threats can have an impact on all aspects of a company's business, from its e-reputation to its production capabilities, to the protection of its assets and even the safety of its personnel.

The constant development of information technologies is a very important source of growth for this entire society. But the interconnection of information systems and the development of online services carry a growing risk: cyberattacks are always more numerous and their impact is stronger and stronger. Their stakes today go beyond the framework of the company and often reach those of the States, whereas the question of the theft of intellectual property and technology feeds the international tensions, in particular with China (The IP chapter, 2020), that the governments seize - more or less openly and legally - business data and the vulnerability of vital infrastructures, many of which are managed by private operators, are of concern to Nations. The risk, however, is primarily assumed by companies and it is unavoidable.

Recently, attacks aimed at sabotaging industrial installations made their public appearance. For example, ARAMCO (The register, 2012), which was attacked in August 2012, has publicly stated that it had to scrap thirty thousand computers. By estimating the replacement of each PC at a thousand dollars, the direct (and public ...) impact of this attack would be thirty million dollars. These significant amounts show that cyber risk has become significant for companies. The risks to SCADA systems are of particular concern to operators of sometimes vital industrial infrastructures because of their potentially dramatic consequences. Yet, despite the existence and maturity of analytical methods, the cyber risk remains insufficiently integrated into the overall analysis of business risks.

The terms cybersecurity or security of information systems are often used to refer to issues or technical measures whose expertise and management are primarily based. While system protection measures are essential, they cannot guarantee absolute security. The increasing probability, the scale and the constant innovation that characterize the attacks mean that, whatever the measures adopted, some risk will persist. Risk is measured by the impact of attacks on a company's business and goals. Too restrictive protections can also hurt a company's production, responsiveness and creativity. The threats thus have a relative value according to their stakes, and their assessment therefore depends on the strategic management of the company. It is therefore essential to define how the company can reduce the risk but also what level of risk it can support (resilience, cost-benefit evaluation ...), what part of the share it can transfer to a third party (insurance ...) and especially how should they handle it in a comprehensive approach. This reflection falls within the strategic domain and therefore the leadership at the highest level of the company which, all too often, abandons it to its technical direction. Certain specificities of cyber risk make it possible to explain it.

The impacts of cyberattacks can be divided into two categories:

direct impacts consist of clean-up of the attack and reclamation of the information system (IS), operating losses and data loss, data theft (strategic decisions, patents, company financial data, ongoing trade negotiations, etc.), and personal data (which leads to direct notification costs) while Indirect impacts lead to image loss, internal and external communication costs, and crisis management.

The risks associated with cyberspace, which are therefore important for a vital infrastructure operator, must be taken into account, like all other risks to an organization (natural disaster, fire risk, civil liability, etc.). Although important, this cyber risk is inherently difficult to quantify precisely. First, the costs of an attack are not easy to evaluate. Moreover, there is no standardized calculation method that would make it possible to obtain consensual statistics on the average cost of this sort of attack. As a result, the return on investment of security solutions is difficult to calculate and the budgets devoted to computer security are considered dry expenses that need to be constantly reduced. Moreover, just because there are threats and vulnerabilities does not mean that they will be exploited and is systematically a risk. Risk apprehension requires a detailed understanding, at different levels of analysis, of the context in which the actor operates and therefore a global vision of the company and its economic and geopolitical environment.

Numerous methods of cyber risk analysis emerged in the early 1980s (Rebecca Slayton, 2015) and have since been developed into very mature products. Thus, in 1982, the Dutch government launched a cyber security risk analysis method (Dutch A & K Analysis, 1996). Since then, many governments have published their analysis tool (s): EBIOS in France (ANSSI, 2019), CRAMM in the UK (Zeki Yazar, 2002), SP800-30 in the US (enisa, 2019), and I-Grundschutz in Germany (enisa, 2019). Beyond these national methods, the ISO 2700X standard is today internationally recognized. ISO 27005 part provides an overall schema that shows how to effectively implement a business risk analysis method. In addition, these methods are equipped and it is not only a question of lists of risks to be covered, but the methods are accompanied by risk calculation formulas, their impact and the priorities to be given to them (MEHARI method for example), (CLUSIF, 2019). Thus, after thirty years of development and international recognition, the cyber risk analysis has reached a certain maturity.

Since the appearance of the first cyberattacks, many protection solutions have been developed by the industry. Antivirus, firewall, security architecture (setting up DMZ Demilitarized Zone., Subnets segmentation for example), but also encryptions, VPN Virtual Private Network., Strong authentication means like the MFA authentication multi-factor, are the necessary bricks to secure the communication networks. More recently, new tools have been designed to detect more sophisticated attacks: IDS / IPS probes, Intrusion Detection System / Intrusion Protection System., SIEM Security Information and Event Management, allowing for the collection and correlation events revealing that an attack is in progress. Despite the excellent performance of these tools, their implementation will not be enough to eliminate cyber risk for several reasons:

- Companies and administrations, targeted by cyberattacks, are increasingly visible (websites, many Internet access, nomadic employees who travel with their computers as BYOD and PDAs) and increasingly rich (information, trade secrets), making them always more attractive to attackers.
- The number of flaws exploitable by attackers is increasing, according to the mechanism described in the previous paragraph
- Too much security kills security. Indeed, if security procedures are stacked, the information system becomes virtually unusable and users bypass the measures in place. This is a riskier situation that makes the company wrongly feels protected

- In the same way, too closed systems would hinder the growth and reactivity of the company, which would penalize its competitiveness. It is therefore, necessary to find a good balance between openness, ease of use and security
- The excellent performance of security solutions is accompanied by a real complexity of management and parameterization. Making them work effectively requires very specialized skills that an organization often has difficulty putting in place: a scarcity of profiles, jobs that are not central to the company's activity, etc.

Cyberattacks seem inevitable despite effective protection solutions. They take place and will continue to take place regularly. The goal must be to reduce their impact to the maximum and develop resilience and business continuity capabilities in the face of this unavoidable risk.

As with risk analysis methods, continuity and disaster recovery plans following a failure of information systems are common. However, the discovery of a cyberattack plunges the company into a deep crisis despite the existence of these plans. Indeed, decision-makers often discovered cyber risk on this occasion and are not prepared to react. This often leads to bad cascading decisions (cutting off all Internet access, for example) that further complicate crisis resolution and the cleaning up of the attack. As for the fire risk, evacuation drills are mandatory every six months. Why not do cyber exercises the same way? This could then be the resilience of the business and the business continuity procedures. ARAMCO, during the attack of August 2012, could only work with faxes for 15 days. This could have been avoided if the company had had better resilience, better business continuity procedures and well-compartmentalised communication networks. Thus, as for the risk analysis, it is not the absence but the lack of knowledge of the plans and the lack of practice that penalize the company. Better internal dialogue would improve the situation. It is all that more necessary that the possibility of outsourcing the risk remains, for the moment, very limited.

Even where decision-makers have developed a common approach to integrating cyber risk into the overall risk analysis, a major step remains to be taken. It is the role of insurance companies that bear the risks of their clients for a premium depending on the risk exposure, the potential impacts as well as the historicity of the claims (sinister). There are indeed structural obstacles to the development of cyber insurance. The European Network Information Security Agency-Enisa and European Union Agency for Cybersecurity identified a few that would justify the difficulty of an effective insurance model (Konstantinos MOULINOS, Enisa, 2019), including:

- The lack of reliable and independent statistics on the impacts of cyber-attacks;
- Since cyber risks are very diverse (loss of personal data versus shutdown of production lines, for example), the insurance market may be very fragmented or unclear as to what is covered;
- As technology evolves rapidly, past and current risks do not predict future risks;
- The absence of reinsurers and insurers of last resort;
- The difficulty for insurers to evaluate the effectiveness of the measures in place to prevent/protect cyber-attacks on their clients;
- The perception that current insurance products already cover all or part of cyber risk.

In addition, a customer who has taken out cyber insurance may become less vigilant and engage in risky behavior (for example, stop for antivirus updates). The insurer, not knowing if his client may neglect his security, will not be able to calculate the amount of the premium. The transfer of risk, therefore, cannot be total.

Typology of threats

Threats to industrial systems come from phenomena as well natural acts, malicious acts and accidents, irregular procedures or technical failures. Historically, these threats have only concerned internal elements of the industrial system in question, including staff members, the organization of facility operators or technical support personnel. However, autonomous worms which randomly search for propagation paths, or (DDoS) viruses (including Trojans), terrorism, disruptions to public services, noise on power lines, electromagnetic interference (EMI) and radio frequency interference (RFI), plant shut down for maintenance and start-up after maintenance (from many harmful events occur during shutdown and startup), improper application of software patches or interdependence with other networks and support items are also serious threats to CI.

The threats of attacks targeting critical infrastructure have multiple dimensions. The following sections break these threats down according to their nature (physical or cybernetics), their origin (internal or external) and the context in which they arise (single or multiple targets). Understanding the different types of threats to critical infrastructure is a first step on the way to developing adequate protection strategies.

Physical threats that target critical infrastructure can take many forms. They have the common characteristic of seeking to destroy, weaken or destroy infrastructure making it totally or partially inoperative by intervening, for example, in its structure physical or mechanical components. The most intuitive physical threats targeting critical infrastructure involve the use of explosives or incendiary devices, means of transport, rockets, systems air defense portable devices (MANPADS), grenades and even simple tools (for example, matches or lighters used to light arson), in particular, the objective being to cause the total or partial collapse or the destruction of infrastructure. Attacks can also materialize through modification or intentional manipulation of the operating systems of critical infrastructures (that are, for example, the starting and stopping of installations, the opening and closing of piping systems or the removal of process signaling systems, signals failure or alarms). The deployment of weapons or chemical, biological substances, is also a special type of threat to infrastructure critics. It can range from the spread of infectious pathogens in chains of food supply and water pipes, for example, to the use of toxic gases at busy crossroads. It should also be noted that the attack on a critical installation containing chemical, biological, radiological or nuclear materials could also result in the release of these materials. Although different, cyber threats and physical threats can produce the same results. Cyber threats, which are variable, can give a lead to attacks consisting, for example, of:

- manipulate systems or data - this is the case with malware exploit vulnerabilities in computer software and hardware components necessary for the operation of critical infrastructure;
- interrupting vital systems - case of saturation attacks;
- restrict access to vital systems or information - for example using ransomware.

If the interconnected computerized control systems and integration have considerably streamlined the way critical infrastructure works and brought about efficiency gains in the market, the extension of connectivity can also broaden the attack surface and expose this infrastructure to a high risk of manipulation.

In a 2010 survey of 200 executives from the private electricity sector in fourteen countries, almost half of those interviewed said that they had never faced saturation attacks or large-scale network infiltrations. In 2011, the situation had considerably improved: 80% of those questioned had had to face an attack by saturation on a large scale, while 85% had been victims of network infiltrations (McAfee, 2011).

Top 10 threats to industrial control systems

Table 4: Top 10 threats to industrial control systems (McAfee, 2011)

Level	Threat	Description
1	Unauthorized use of access points remote maintenance	The access points for maintenance are external inputs to the network of industrial control systems, intentionally created and often insufficiently secure.
2	Online attacks via office networks or companies	For connection to networks, office computer systems usually use multiple channels. In most cases, since there are also connections network between offices and industrial control systems, attackers can gain access through this route.
3	Attacks on standard components used in networks control systems industrial	Standard IT components, such as software operating systems, application servers or databases often have flaws or vulnerabilities that can be exploited by pirates. If these standard components are also used in the network of industrial

		control systems, the risk of a successful attack on this network increased.
4	Saturation Attacks	Overrun attacks can harm network connections and vital resources and cause systems to crash, the goal consisting, for example, in disrupting the functioning of a industrial control.
5	Human error and sabotage	Intentional acts - whether committed by internal actors or external - pose a significant threat to all objectives protective measures. Negligence and human error also constitute significant threats, particularly with regard to protection objectives of confidentiality and availability.
6	Introduction of malicious software via removable media and external hardware	The use of removable media and computer components mobile by external personnel always carries a high risk malware infection
7	Reading and registration of the information in the network systems industrial	Since most control components use currently plain text protocols, communications are not protected. It is thus relatively easy to read and enter control commands.

	controls	
8	Unauthorized access to resources	The task turns out to be particularly easy for attackers interns or those who carry out attacks after a first external penetration if the services and components of the network processes do not use authentication methods and authorization or if the methods implemented are not secure.
9	Attacks on standard components	Attackers can manipulate the components of a network, for example to carry out interceptor attacks or to facilitate network sniffing.
10	Malfunctions techniques or force majeure.	Power outages caused by conditions of extreme weather or technical failures can occur at any time - in such cases, they can only limit as much as possible the risks and potential damage. (OSCE, 2014)

If the protection of critical infrastructures against external attacks benefits from an extensive volume of directives from national and international regulatory bodies, the threats posed by internal actors are given less attention. Compared to external actors, who can only access critical infrastructure through violence or by stratagems, internal authors enjoy indisputable advantages. It's about often employees or suppliers of these companies, which can be the main conspirators or act as accomplices (for example, as informants) of actors exteriors.

They are often able to observe the processes for some time without being disturbed. Their knowledge (or the ease with which they can acquire knowledge) relating to the relevant facilities can be easily exploited for criminal purposes.

With this in mind, the risk assessment methods that weigh on specific sites should take into account each function within the system and the vulnerabilities linked to the internal actors should not be considered as a separate category. Instead and place, it is necessary to examine the different types of threats by including, in each category, an "internal player" element. For example, when looking at a threat category such as that of an improvised attack, the assessors should separately analyze the case of an attack carried out by an external threat and that of an improvised attack carried out by employees. In this case, operators of the concerned infrastructures can play a key preventive role, starting with effective control procedures for staff selection.

Threats to critical infrastructure can either translate into action isolated and sporadic or as part of larger plans to attack infrastructure that is part of the same sector (for example, power plants nuclear), belonging to the same owner or operator or is located in the same geographical area. This can very well place terrorist actions targeting infrastructure critics on the same level as industrial espionage, which often leads to the launching of cyberattacks in the form of "campaigns" or serial attacks. For example, in 2011, the so-called "LURID" APT attack (Roger A. Grimes, 2011) notably targeted the computer systems of several diplomatic missions and government space agencies. Identifying trends in similar scenarios often requires tools powerful analytics and processing of information from multiple sources and heterogeneous. To further complicate matters, as the OSCE points out in the energy sector, most cyberattacks are not made public because the operators concerned are reluctant to report these incidents. However, the ability to recognize the dynamics and underlying methods as early as possible contributes in a way decisive for responsible authorities to exchange information in real-time, which gives more ways to react more effectively to ongoing attacks and to anticipate imminent attacks likely to provoke victims (OSCE report, 2013). In some cases, what may appear to be an isolated attack on relatively "unimportant" targets is likely to be part of more ambitious and criminal strategies, constantly evolving: EDS, Advanced Persistent Threat Activity Targeting Energy and Other Critical Infrastructure Sectors (CERT 2017).

Because of the heterogeneous nature of critical infrastructures and also the diversity of their geographic and institutional frameworks, it seems extremely difficult to conclude what motivates terrorists or hacker activists to carry out attacks against these infrastructures rather than against non-critical targets. The fact remains that the analysis of terrorist motivations could suggest useful leads as part of the overall threat assessments that required national strategies for protecting critical infrastructure. Limited empirical research in this area (Ackerman, 2007) reveals that, for various reasons, critical infrastructure has a certain appeal. First, they can be attractive targets because of their strategic value to companies, especially those from the highly industrialized countries of the Western Hemisphere. Disrupting the functioning of critical infrastructure, preferably by provoking a reactions chain, allows them to maximize damage in a single operation and instill fear at levels they could not reach as easily when attacking "Ordinary" Targets. Other critical infrastructures can be targeted to demonstrate the powerlessness of state institutions. For example, terrorist or activist organizations may decide to attack power plants or pipelines to interrupt the provision of basic services and highlight the fragility of public bodies and government policies (Ackerman 2007, p. 170). A third possible motivation, linked to the previous two, would be the desire to reach a higher level of publicity than one could target by focusing on low visibility. In many cases, there is likely to be a combination of factors that lead to attacks on critical infrastructure. These incentives are offset by several constraints. The final decision as to which infrastructure to target will depend on the operational capabilities of a group to launch a given attack. The protection measures implemented in an infrastructure Criticism given will naturally influence this decision. It does not follow that hackers attack critical infrastructure only when they are sure they can disrupt its operation. A simple attempt, even if it fails or causes very limited damage, can provide the desired media impact, especially when the target is chosen for its symbolic value.

Cyberattack seriously challenges the fundamental elements of the rule of law, the protection of human rights and their effective application. As part of the obligations incumbent on them under international human rights law, States must protect the people under their jurisdiction from any infringement of their rights fundamentals by third parties, including terrorist actors. This obligation has of particular importance, given the potential impact that attacks against critical infrastructure can have on populations, given the role that these infrastructures often play in maintaining or carrying out vital societal functions. The disruption or destruction of critical infrastructures or the damage inflicted on them can have far-reaching implications for a wide range of human rights, ranging from the right to life and security of the person to the right to health and a healthy environment, to the right to education, water, sanitation and other aspects of the right to a decent standard living.

Critical infrastructures and Industrial Systems often use standard Internet connection gateways that are very sensitive to cyber threats. However, security mechanisms to protect infrastructure must not disrupt the critical operations upon which the societies rely. This results in many challenges for managing cybersecurity critical infrastructures.

Data Acquisition and Control Systems (SCADA) and Industrial Control Systems (ICS) are the cornerstones of critical infrastructures. SCADA networks have been designed to provide robust performance, reliability, flexibility and distributed control security, while unfortunately neglecting the cybersecurity side of critical infrastructures. SCADA networks are vulnerable to service interruptions, process redirection, and operational data manipulation. A cyberattack can lead to public safety problems or serious disruption of States or companies critical infrastructures. Among the threats, critical infrastructures, especially the energy sector, has reported an increased incidence of Advanced Persistent Threats (APTs) which are attack techniques involving injection, SQL, XSS, etc. Add to the problem, the fact that it is difficult to detect a compromised system. Hackers can access a system and advance masked by masquerading as a trusted employee for long periods.

APT uses a whole arsenal of attack techniques and tools to achieve its goal, the components of such an attack are not necessarily technically "advanced" (phishing, malware, XSS, etc.). Tools for generating attack components exist (e.g. Poison Ivy, etc.). But the combination of attack methods and tools makes it an advanced attack. However, it is an attack whose impact must be feared because it is based on a strategy whose objective is to stay as long as possible without arousing suspicion (stealth), by contrast, It is an "Opportunistic" Attack. It is scripted by the attackers, and specific goals are established to compromise a whole chain of systems; fallback targets can be defined. And its main objective is to stay under "radars" ("low and slow ") while attacking critical infrastructure.

So it is of course a serious threat against CIs, it implies coordination of technical means and humans and is generally poorly automated (although system compromises can be). Attackers are highly motivated and equipped with skills, unusual techniques and means and are distinguished from traditional attacks by their "weak signals" but their major impact (Low-frequency & high-impact), by the fact that they are based on objectives and a strategy (no improvisation), by their sophisticated techniques used, and by their need for coordination between the hackers who lead them. They require good technical skills and the attack must remain stealthy (not generating noise). The financial or industrial gain from these attacks is not immediate but has the advantage of lasting until the objective is reached. In the case of information theft and infiltration, this attack can take a very long time. They have a significant cost:

- Exit script-kiddies and hackers looking for notoriety.
- A priori they are orchestrated by organized crime, militant groups, even States.

These particular infrastructures, the preservation and functioning of which are essential for national security and the continuity of societal functions, face a real threat.

Critical infrastructures such as power plants and power grids, oil pipelines, airports and railway stations can be damaged, interrupted or destroyed by deliberate acts (APT attacks, DDoS attacks, etc.), or natural disasters (negligence, accident), because of criminal activities or malicious acts. As these infrastructures often operate in an interdependent and complex network, and belong to a large number of public and private sectors, it is necessary to structure and coordinate the protection of these so-called "critical" infrastructures between the governments, the public, and private sectors.

DESIGN &
SECURITY PLATFORM

As SCADA networks are a set of computer hardware and applications used to control and monitor vital infrastructure, Computer information networks are curtailed to the success of conveyance of data packets and resource sharing, in both minute and ambiguous networks. It connects people, supports applications and services, and provides channels and access to resources that keep the transport session running. This implies the need for the development of a functional and efficient network for secure and reliable network communication and the conveyance of packets across the organization's network. It is therefore required to design around the SCADA networks, a secure network infrastructure able to manage and meet different criteria that are needed for the configuration of the network devices. Security is to provide and ensure that all the network traffic is working properly and to keep track of the communication channel by avoiding unauthorized access, exploitation and modification of the network resources. Without laying up a professional network security configuration, any organization is exposed to various multiple threats that the attackers pose to the network channel. Hence it is essential to set up a combined strict and firm Networking rules and Risk management.

Designing Networking

Today's SCADA systems are now networked and can communicate over a wide area network (WAN) over data lines or over the phone which means more vulnerabilities. That's why network infrastructure needs to be seriously considered while building SCADA networks. Network Infrastructure is the key component such as software or hardware that makes the computer operate smoothly through the network and its trafficking. In operation and management of the communication, path and all the networking services are governed by several application services that lay the foundation between the user and the external network or the internet as a whole.

However, establishing the communication can lead to a Sniffing Attack: a threat that can be used by the intruders for entering the network and steal sensitive data, an Application Layer Attack: which consists of injecting various types of malicious codes, Man in the Middle Attack (MITM): which consists of the attacker interfering between communicants to intercept and transfer any reply through the IPsec protocol suite, and Flooding Attack: It's a simple but significantly destructive attack, they rely on web servers responding to an attacker's requests falsely, deemed legitimate. The attacker sends a very high volume of traffic to a system to saturate it, the system suffocates and stops responding to a rather legitimate request; the web then stops working and crashes. This is known as Death by Saturation or as Denial of Service (DoS) Attacks.

To ensure a successfully designed network, all the network devices need to be set up and configured to the requirement needed for communication and must be able to support the amount of traffic that is needed to be conveyed across the entire network. The network is categorized within different characteristics as follow: Local Area Network (LAN) which connects various computers and devices in a given limited geographical area such as libraries and departments, Wide Area Network (WAN) that covers an intensively larger geographical area such as State, town, and region, Metropolitan Area Network (MAN) which is a relatively larger network that covers a span of a city or maybe large campuses, and Personal Area Network (PAN) a computer network used to communicate with other computers which have different information technology devices like fax machines, printers, and telephones.

On every given network there is always a design issue that may arise such as choosing the best possible channel between the sender and the receiver when more than one route is found and are available for package transfer, ensuring the rate of sending and the rate of receiving are intact and match. If the rate of sending is too high, it overtakes the rate at which the receiver gets it and consumes the packets then leads to data loss and congestion of data traffic. In this case, flow control can be used:

The sender and receiver identification should be made possible for each of the layers and the addressing of each can make it easier for them to communicate.

Another major issue is the maximum size of data that can be sent and received once at a given time which may lead to the need for segmentation at the sender and assembly at the receiver. The data transfer rules determine the number of channels needed and the priorities been used, by using the mode of communication as Simplex, half-duplex and full-duplex.

When designing a network many designers come across complex complicated mixed application protocols, devices, and linked technologies. The process may involve many feasibility connections, each with different attributes and different costs. Network Design Tools analyzes what is happening in the given network and predicts future behaviors and happenings. The use of designing tools depends on:

- The conception of the ideal network,
- The general purpose in which the tool predicts ink and devices throughput and the utilization of the network,
- The effects of links or device failure,

- Which links and devices are over and underused, and also on how unbalanced loads affects links and devices,
- Changes in topology devices upgrades or expansion which may affect performance and to model the LAN, frame and every relay, and IP as Compuware's CommNet III, Eco Predictor, and Eco Profiler.

Some departments may need to be configured to use and share a printer or/and other connected devices, and every department needs to have an FTP server that is managed by the Information Technology (IT) department. Any department's web server needs to be managed by IT and all the laptops and mobiles can only be accessed whilst external with a secure VPN. The network must be divided into a distinctive layer type whereby each layer performs a discrete function. There are many different networking design models out there to choose from.

The Hierarchical Networking design with a simple network laydown of switches on a flat network would be appropriate (as a standard) for a well-secured network. It's a little undesirable type of network model since it provides and gives limited opportunity to broadcast or even to filter different undesirable network traffic (Hsu, F. and Marinucci, D. 2012), because of the nodes connected to the flat network. The downside of this networking is that its response time is degraded. However, this model has a huge advantage as it performs various functions in the organization and divides the flat network into three separate types of broadcasting domains as follow:

- Core Layer – provides faster conveyance of data packets from the switch to the router
- Distribution Layer – provides policy-based configuration of various controls and the boundary between the core and access
- Access Layer – provides workgroup/user connectivity for the network of host and end devices

Only traffic destined for other networks is moved to a higher layer and WAN needs some types of data link protocol to concrete a communication link between the sender and the receiving node.

Data is conveyed from the data Link Layer on the physical link which in any scenario is a point to point on a WAN connection. The frame around the specified network layer in the data link can check and control the specified network and other functions if applied in the communication channel. For a single WAN connectivity type, it uses a Layer 2 protocol to encapsulate a packet while it conveys the WAN link. For a proper encapsulation, the layer 2 type must be used in each router serial interface and must be configured; given an example, when a recipient makes a phone call, the dialed number is used to set switches in the trade along the path of the call so that there is a continuous end to end Communication Layer of the circuit from the caller to the recipient party.

Because of the various switching techniques and general network operations used to establish the circuit, the telephone communication system is called a circuit-switched network. If the telephones are replaced with modems, then the switched circuit can convey computer data packets. Packet switching divides data traffic into packets that are routed over a shared channel network. Packet switching networks do not need a circuit to finalize the communication.

The switches in a packet-switched network are used to vary which link in the packet must be conveyed on as the next from the addressing information in each packet, while WAN connection links are conveyed through given dedicated broadband services such as DSL and cable modem that are combined with VPN technology which is used to provide data privacy (confidentiality) across the Internet. VLAN offers efficient use and benefits significantly in terms of bandwidth flexibility, performance and security.

Frame ware is often cheaper as compared to point-to-point, particularly when connecting within different sites with the increase of distance.

Nevertheless, its dedication capacity removes latency between various endpoints, and its constant availability is essential for various applications such as VoIP or Video over.

Three main objectives need to be attained while setting up network security: Confidentiality, Integrity, and Availability. However, When it comes to network consideration appliances, it is essential to consider ethical Network security and legal network security (Zhang, et al. 2012).

Risk management

Risk management goes through several stages, it involves understanding the risk, by analyzing the process, the physical hazard and the characteristics of the social body under threat (the notion of vulnerability), as well as its reactions to the eventual accident; knowing the risk requires assessing the return time of the hazard by considering the frequency and intensity of past events. It is also a question of foreseeing the possible manifestations of the hazard, to reducing its impact by adapted facilities or by the management of the appropriate space. It is essential to prevent disaster by planning policies. There are three types of Risk Management: Forecasting, Protection, and Prevention. They involve education and information of those in charge to protect others.

For the protection of premises, A Physical Access Control policy should be defined. This policy should include:

- Recover the keys or badges (if any) of an employee at his departure and regularly changing the access codes of the building such as the alarm.
- Never give a key or alarm code to external service providers unless it is possible to trace the accesses and restrict them to ranges given hours.

- Buildings access points should be protected.
- Access to the premises should be logged and auditable.
- Access control mechanisms should be robust.
- Access to equipment should be restricted to authorized persons.
- Access should be video protected.
- An intrusion detection system will have to be implemented for the zones vital, especially those not occupied 24 hours a day.
- Servers should be installed in enclosed, controlled premises access (if possible in computer rooms).
- Station CPUs, industrial network equipment and PLCs should be placed in locked cabinets.
- Access to the system should not be accessible to the public and access to the industrial system should not be accessible in no monitoring areas.
- When not in use, the plugs dedicated to maintenance should be plugged out (plugs, blackout plates, etc.).
- The removal of the shutter follows a well-defined procedure and is subject to prior authorization.
- The physical integrity of the cables should be protected (for example a rollover).
- An opening detection device, with alarm escalation, should be set up on the cabinets of sensitive equipment.
- At a minimum, on external cabinets containing sensitive components, a means of control visual, such as the installation of seals for example should be installed.
- The withdrawal of these visual aids should follow a well-defined procedure and be subject to preliminary authorization.

It is also important to note that the human being is at the first line of the defense against critical infrastructures cyber threats, the human being helps set the tone for his approach to information security, as such, the user must consider it in its broadest sense, not just in terms of information technology.

Information security encompasses a combination of people, processes and technologies and therefore does not only concern information technologies, the implementation of security measures should not be the fact of only computer services but should touch all the activities of the organization. The perimeter of information security, therefore, extends to the resources, human resources, products, facilities, processes, policies, procedures, systems, technologies, equipment, networks and data.

If the results collected during the investigation mentioned above are transposed, it would be obvious that the human is the backdoor key to the attackers but also the key that prevents them from entering the system covets if simple rules are followed.

Indeed, Identifying and managing the vulnerabilities of informational assets and the threats involved can be a huge task. During my professional life as an IT Support, I came across some explosive numbers; 35% of security incidents result from human error rather than deliberate attack (and that was sometimes ago, I believe today some experts are talking about 45% to 50%. However, I don't have the data to confirm this), and more than half of the remaining incidents are due to attacks that could have been avoided if the information had been processed more securely. It is also obvious that the lack of training of employees is a security gap for critical facilities.

The Logical Access Controls must be set as capable of managing all different types of accounts:

- Session accounts allowing access to Windows and Linux machines;
- The Application accounts allowing a participant to connect to a SCADA application for example. These accounts are often managed by the application itself;
- The System accounts used for an application to run

and communicate with other applications (example: service account). These accounts are not normally used by a stakeholder. Accounts can have different levels of privileges.

In particular, Administrator Level Accounts fall into two categories:
- The high privileges accounts, system administrator allowing the IT administration of equipment (servers, stations and equipment network for example) and operating systems;
- High privilege accounts is a "process engineer" allowing access to configuration or programming functions of SCADA applications and automata for example.

It should be noted however that for reasons of convenience, accounts are often mixed while they should be well separated. A "Process Engineer" has not yet need to be a System Administrator. This is a bad practice:

- Each user should be uniquely identified.
- All accounts with important privileges such as accounts administrators should be protected by an authentication mechanism like a password.
- User and administrator accounts should be strictly separated be uniquely identified, and those that are generic accounts, especially those with significant privileges, are deprecated. When indispensable, their use should be limited to specific uses very accurate and be documented.
- Roles should be defined, documented and implemented so that user accounts have privileges exactly matching their missions.
- And the audit of the events related to the use of the accounts should be in place.
- Accounts owned by staff no longer interfere with the

system industrial site or company should be deleted or, at least, deactivated. But to avoid errors, it is almost a must that these unused accounts be deleted.

- Default and generic accounts should not be used unless constrained by strong operations.
- Accounts with privileges such as accounts administrators should not be generic accounts and should be separate from the user accounts.
- Accounts with privileges must be validated by the hierarchical manager of the user.
- An annual review of user accounts should be put in place.

This review may, in particular, help to verify the correct application of the guidelines and this review should pay particular attention to the administrative accounts. Where possible, read-only access should be configured for first-level maintenance interventions.

If account management is centralized, the configuration of the centralized directory should be audited regularly and at least once a year, better twice. For the Active Directory Case,

A Centralized Solution can facilitate the management of accounts and rights of stakeholders. This kind of solution can also create a single point of vulnerability and therefore needs to be studied with the utmost care.

CHAPTER 2

- ❖ Operation of SCADA Systems
- ❖ Means of access to an attack
     to SCADA systems
- ❖ Cyber-Physical Attack
- ❖ Availability Attacks
- ❖ Confidentiality Attacks
- ❖ Integrity Attacks
- ❖ Identifying Vulnerability
- ❖ System Protection

OPERATION OF
SCADA SYSTEMS

Critical infrastructures protection includes all activities aimed at preventing, mitigating or neutralizing the risk for a reduction or discontinuity in the availability of supplies or services essential for the safeguarding of vital interests or essential needs of all or part of the Country and its population. Critical infrastructures protection is therefore aimed at activities of vital importance, essential for the proper functioning of socio-economic life, in all sectors and against all potential risks. The field of protection of critical infrastructure includes a national component, a European, or/and an international component. Indeed, the consequences of the destruction or cessation of critical infrastructure may be limited to one country, or affect two or more countries due to the interdependence of transnational networks. It is therefore essential to protect these highly interdependent infrastructures, both at a national and global level: the level of security of each State depends on the security provided by other States.

Although their implementation is often proprietary, SCADA controllers are essentially small computers, they use standard IT elements such as operating system (Windows or Unix, often embedded), software applications, accounts and connections, communication protocols, etc. In addition, some of the management environments are standard Windows and Unix workstations. Consequently, the well-known problems of vulnerability also apply to the SCADA and ICS systems, with the additional problem of the difficulty of physically accessing these systems or the impossibility of stopping their operation.

Contrary to common belief, SCADA and ICS networks are generally not physically separated from computer networks. Some companies, however, have separate LANs or separate their corporate network from their control network. In other cases, businesses use the same local and Wide Area Network, but encrypt SCADA and ICS traffic in the shared infrastructure. More frequently, however, networks require a certain level of interconnections to obtain operational commands and export data to third-party external systems. SCADA network equipment has specific characteristics that can be very different from traditional computer systems:

- They are often installed in hard-to-reach places (for example, in towers, oil platforms and industrial machinery) and have different environmental constraints than standard computer systems (e.g. outdoor operation, extreme temperatures, vibrations). or require input voltages and special assemblies.
- They often use proprietary operating systems that are not enhanced.
- Their software cannot be updated or corrected frequently because of access difficulties, probable downtime or the need to re-certify them.
- They use proprietary or special protocols.

These different environments create problems such as lack of authentication and encryption, and weak password storage that allows hackers to access systems. Even though most SCADA / ICS networks have some level of defense at their perimeter, including network segmentation and firewall technologies, attackers are still looking for other ways to penetrate the network from the inside, for example, through a backdoor or by triggering actions from inside the company to open a communication channel with the outside. Typical attack scenarios are:

- Using a remote access port usually reserved for a maintenance service provider
- Piracy of a legitimate channel between computer systems and SCADA / ICS systems
- Convince an internal user to click on a link in an email from a workstation connected to the SCADA / ICS network and the Internet
- Infecting laptops and / or removable media outside the SCADA / ICS network and then infecting internal systems when they connect to the network to collect data, update the controller / sensors, etc.
- Exploit security configuration errors or connected devices.

A hacker who has successfully infiltrated a SCADA network can send malicious commands to block or break devices, and interfere with the specific critical processes they control, such as opening and closing valves.

ACCESS MEANS
TO ATTACK SCADA SYSTEMS

Today all industrial systems are connected to the Internet, to different corporate networks, public switched telephone networks, satellites and wireless communication systems (WIFI, WiMax). However, attackers can also use:

- Business or Corporate Networks,
- Connections to other networks that contain vulnerabilities,
- Compromised Virtual Private Networks (VPN),
- Connections by Backdoor through remote access modems,
- Unsecured wireless connections discovered by users of portable like BYOD and PDA,
- Open computer ports, such as UDP or TCP ports that are not unnecessarily protected or opened.

They can also use weak authentication in protocols and system components industrial, maintenance phishing (maintenance hooks) or doors trap doors, which are ways to bypass controls security during industrial system development, and Buffer Overflow Attacks on System Control Servers Industrial, accessible by Automata and Man-Machine Interfaces (MMI), to penetrate a vulnerable system.

After gaining access to the industrial system, the attacker seeks at all costs to obtain a certain level of control of its components, depending on the protections associated with each component, the attacker visibility and to the latter abilities and intentions. The realization of one or more cyber threats within an industrial system can therefore have consequences such as data disclosure sensitive, material damage to property and people, risks of public health and damage to image and reputation. This is why the legal issues of Cyber Security of Industrial Systems must be taken very seriously.

CYBER-PHYSICAL
SYSTEMS ATTACK

Cyber-physical systems (CPS) integrate computer and communication capabilities into traditional production environments. The use of Supervisory Control And Data Acquisition (SCADA) technologies plays an important role in the construction of critical infrastructures with CPS at the national level. Cyber-Physical Attacks can disrupt these systems, putting people's safety, environmental regulation and industrial work at risk.

A CPS is a system that monitors physical entities, taking measures to control and/or correct their behavior. They can be modelled in the form of a Networked Control System (NCS). Cyber-Physical Attacks are these attacks perpetrated especially against automaton Programmable Logic Controllers (PLC), the Human-Machine Interface (HMI) and their infrastructure and can deliberately interrupt production or destroy equipment to stop the business activities and cause financial loss and reputation, are Cyber-Physical Attacks against the Control and Acquisition Data Systems (SCADA) and Process Control or Distributed Control Systems (DCS). They aimed to compromise the safety of the employees and neighbouring communities.

These attacks, when they are led by activists with no political motivation or no interest in harming a State to the benefit of another State, may simply be those of stealing confidential information on product revenues to reveal trade secrets to competitors, and help the purchasers to know everything about the operating process of their competitor products. This method is due to harms the efficiency and productivity of a business and weakens its competitive advantage.

However, such attacks on critical infrastructure are very rare. Attacking the State owed vital infrastructure is of great interest and hackers/attackers should not be limited simply to the resale of products to competitors. Hence, special attention to vital infrastructure must be increased because these attacks often have a specific purpose; do the maximum damage to employees, and civilians, and spread terror and fear among the population.

With the development of the Internet of Things (IoT) and the Amazon Web Service (AWS) cloud, the interconnection of systems and the associated cybercrime risks are becoming increasingly important. This requires a specific approach to Industrial Control Systems (ICS) traditionally subject to the risk of confidential data theft. They stand out from traditional information systems, drive physical installations and operate critical industrial installations. According to the ISA 95 standard, the architecture of an industrial network is organized into 6 levels:

- Level 0 - Terrain: sensors, actuators, motor.
- Level 1 - Process: automata, safety systems, controllers.
- Level 2 - Supervision: SCADA stations.
- Level 3 - Driving: factory driving, MES.
- Level 4 and Level 5 - Business: PC, office, messaging, intranet.

These systems control physical infrastructure through Operational Technologies (OT), so cyberattacks against them will be more numerous and could have much more serious consequences. These attacks focus first on the Availability of data, then on their Integrity and finally on their Confidentiality, while those against conventional networks prioritize Confidentiality first, Integrity second and then the Availability of data.

Attacks targeting ICS systems have progressively improved.

Stuxnet is the first attack to highlight the vulnerability of ICS. Capable of compromising industrial control processes, the malware included several social engineering techniques, applications, file types and vulnerabilities found in Windows and ICS software. For example, in the energy sector, water, electricity, oil and gas, ICS is an ideal target for cybercriminals. The main tasks to be targeted for the attackers to commit their acts of sabotage are the monitoring of temperature, hygrometry, flow rates and uninterrupted power supply. Distributed Control Systems (DCS) are intended for industrial processes whose control elements are distributed or geo-distributed. Unlike centralized control systems that include a single central controller that manages all system control-command functions, Distributed Control Systems or DCS consist of several controllers that control the subsystems or units of the overall installation. Once mastered, all these SCADA Systems allow the user to simulate functions such as moving an object up or down using scripts. To add a button to stop and start, another button to move it more slowly, another to go faster etc ... Most software has a simulation system that simulates the system designed beforehand.

SCADA supervision systems are almost indispensable for medium / large production systems, But one of the criteria involved in the choice of a supervisory system is its resistance to cyberattacks. Indeed, such attacks can have serious consequences. especially in areas such as nuclear power or remote control of subways, telecommunications and health systems and disrupting the daily lives of citizens.

ATTACKS SEEKING
TO INTERRUPT
AVAILABILITY

As already mentioned, critical infrastructure (electricity, oil, gas, water, waste, etc.) relies heavily on electrical, mechanical, hydraulic and other types of equipment. This equipment is controlled and supervised by dedicated computer systems called controllers and sensors. These systems are connected to management systems, and together form networks using SCADA solutions (Remote Monitoring and Data Acquisition System) and ICS (Industrial Control System). SCADA and ICS enable efficient data collection and analysis, and automatic control of equipment such as pumps, valves and relays. The benefits provided by these systems have contributed to their widespread adoption, their robustness and stability allow critical infrastructures to use SCADA and Industrial Control System (ICS) solutions for long periods.

SCADA / ICS networks and devices have been designed to provide maximum reliability and maneuverability. They often do not incorporate security mechanisms to prevent unauthorized access or to cope with ever-evolving security threats from external and internal networks that are prevalent in the computing world.

The security of a system relies on three properties that are confidentiality, integrity and availability and cyber security is itself based on these three main pillars; Each tool deployed and each procedure implemented always responds to at least one of these elements.

But what is a system? A system is an entity that interacts with other entities, so other systems, including hardware, software, humans and the physical world with its natural phenomena.

Historically the majority of efforts have been concentrated on privacy. The army has always wanted to ensure that their communication remains secret, the banks want to ensure professional secrecy and the industry wants to protect its production and keep it secret. There is therefore a lot of research done on cryptographic systems to ensure a certain level of confidentiality in the storage and exchange of information. However, it should be noted that today, hackers are more interested in compromising the availability of data. Indeed, they can hardly make a breach of confidentiality profitable, so they have preferred to prevent access. For example, Ransomware is only intended to block the owner access to its data, or the DDoS Attacks that make a computer system inaccessible. An attack against ICS will make the collection of data unavailable and will stop the control of the equipment mentioned above which ensures the functioning of the SCADA system.

Availability Attacks, which are usually the result of indiscriminate attacks, degrade the operability of a system by reducing the false-positive rate. when the system breaks down in this way, it becomes difficult to act reliably on the results obtained, and the attack is therefore considered as a reduction in the availability of the system. This type of attack is only relevant for so-called Causative Attacks, as it generally involves the manipulation of the decision-making functions of an online learning agent.

Critical infrastructures are also subject to DDoS Attacks. It does not take much to paralyze an entire section of the Internet. a configuration error in a large network infrastructure company can cause failures for several major operators. Even if it is an accident and not an act of malicious intent, the unavailability of a single minute can result in a penalty for operators and their customers.

These types of attacks are:

- Volumetric: these Bandwidth-Intensive Attacks are essentially aimed at "flooding" network links and routers interfaces.
- TCP State Exhaustion: Attacks of this type saturate all Transmission Control Protocol (TCP) connections available on Internet infrastructure equipment such as firewalls, load balancers, and web servers.
- Applicative: These "Sneaky" Attacks are intended to gradually exhaust the resources of the application servers.

In addition, attacks are now much easier to launch by less experienced authors, thanks to the availability of cheap kit tools to rent DDoS services. The threat landscape is further complicated by the rapid proliferation of insufficiently secure equipment within the Internet of Things (IoT), which is being touted as "zombies" in botnets for the launch of Multi-vector DDoS Attacks. In the face of the upsurge of Multi-vector Attacks, the mitigation of the risk of DDoS Attacks requires a defense in depth or at several levels, combining several synchronized neutralization methods. Intelligent DDoS Disabling Solutions (IDMS), specifically designed to counter DDoS Attacks, are deployed on-site, in front of the firewall. These solutions can handle the majority of DDoS Attacks, of which 80% are less than 1 Gbit / s. However, they are not sufficient given the increasing number of large-scale attacks to saturate Internet bandwidth, which is more effective in the cloud. Today's defense best practices are the intelligent integration of on-premise and cloud solutions.

ATTACKS AIMED
AT EXFILTRATING
CONFIDENTIAL DATA

Confidentiality defines the absence of unauthorized disclosure of information. An attack on confidentiality is an attack to attempt to retrieve information for which it does not have permission, either by attempting to access it on the system, by listening to network communications or in any other way possible.

Advanced Persistent Threats, commonly referred to as APTs, are some of the worst threats today; APTs concern States as well as companies and organizations. These cybercriminals are capable of breaking into the information system of their victims to steal sensitive information.

The irreversible tendency of the Bring Your Own Device (BOYD) facilitates the intrusions, the infection of private mobile devices such as tablets, smartphones or MP3s makes it possible to break into their victim's systems to extract data.

APT Attacks

An APT is a **Targeted Attack** that relies on malware that is tailored and able to bypass existing security features. It comes from an association of criminals - no longer isolated hacker - who infiltrates a company to spy on it. An APT always ends with the theft of sensitive data. APT's attackers work hard to keep their actions undetected. They sneak from one compromised host to another, without generating network traffic using spaghetti code (Symantec 2011a). Some hackers mutate the code used, thwarting the security solutions in place to remain undetectable. It is common for an attacked company to realize this only belatedly. An APT is very often sponsored because its execution requires serious computer skills. The performers are perfectly organized. They are very often funded by States (Muller 2014). To achieve their ends, they use a cocktail of very well dosed means: Trojan, for example, unwittingly installed by a reckless user. It consists of exploiting the vulnerabilities of software or a program and setting up various tools for subsequent operations.

The procedure is essentially the same from one attack to another. At first, the users are the main target for hackers, as they will serve as an entry point. APT relies on social engineering and **zero-day** vulnerability (Symantec 2011b). The hacker learns quietly about his target to know them well. It will then be easier for the attacker to convince its potential victims, to click on a link or open an attachment, and once access is obtained, the hacker then tries to increase their privileges. At this stage, the hacker enjoys at least the access rights granted to the legitimate user of the machine he occupies without his knowledge. Exfiltration programs, encryption tools, proxies ... are introduced. The attacker explores the network to reach the data servers. He uses application vulnerabilities, compromised item information and all the mechanisms that will allow him to access new machines with higher access rights and containing the sensitive information he seeks; after this "investigation" runs by him, the exfiltration of the data can then begin. And when the hacker leaves the field of operations, he erases the traces of his passage to always remain perfectly invisible. Here are the steps followed by the hacker to exfiltrate data from potential victims:

- Approach of the victim by social engineering or other means (for example keylogger installed through the http web feed, or through a spear-phishing type mail - particularly targeted phishing email, etc.)
- Stealth infiltration of target systems,
- Establishment of a backdoor after penetration on the network
- Obtaining access rights to other internal systems,
- Installation of a set of tools necessary for clandestinity and exfiltration of data,
- Obtaining greater privileges,
- Discrete and regular exfiltration of data.

Unlike more ordinary cyberattacks, APT campaigns use custom methods based on the target to be attained, rather than more generic tools designed to reach a maximum of victims. APT campaigns usually take longer than ordinary attacks, which are more obvious and therefore easier to counter.Particularly targeted are sectors such as national defense, industry and finance, where information is of paramount importance (intellectual property, military plans and other data from public authorities and companies). Most APTs seek permanent access to the targeted network rather than entering and leaving the network as quickly as possible. Given the efforts and resources to perpetrate APT attacks, hackers choose high-value targets, such as Nation-States and large corporations, with the ultimate goal of stealing information for a long time. To infiltrate, APT groups often adopt Advanced Attack Modes, including "zero-day" vulnerabilities, spear phishing (which is itself a form of advanced phishing that takes the mechanism by customizing them according to the targets to increase the effectiveness) and other social engineering techniques (an attack that relies heavily on human relations to induce a backdoor way to violate security procedures).

To maintain access to the targeted network without being detected, hackers multiply methods. In particular, they must rewrite malicious code constantly and deploy sophisticated concealment techniques. Some APT threats are so complex that compromised systems and software management is a full-time administrator's job.

If supported by Nations, the APT can, for example, seek to steal intellectual property to gain a competitive advantage in certain industries like Energy distribution, telecommunications and other infrastructure systems. But if APT attacks are hard to detect, data theft is never totally invisible. The exfiltration of data, however, could be the only evidence of the attack suffered by a network.

Tools as Backdoors, File Transfer Protocol (FTP), FTP Protocol Vulnerabilities, and others are exploited for attacks:

Backdoors.

This Web-Based Social Engineering Attack relies on malicious Java applets. These applets will install backdoors on Windows, Linux and Mac systems and when users visit the site, they are prompted to run a Java applet whose signature has not been validated by a trusted certificate authority. If the applet is executed, it starts by determining which operating system is running on the connected user's computer and then drops the malicious binary file corresponding to the platform. The goal is then to establish a connection with a command and control the server, and to retrieve other infected codes to download and run them on the compromised computer. The attack uses the Social Engineering Toolkit, a consumer tool designed to test the resilience of systems to intrusions. Backdoors have the ability for executing a very complex code that encrypts data to communicate with other servers. These multi-platform attacks indicate that Linux and Mac OS X are increasingly attractive targets for cybercriminals as it allows malware designers to target more users and spread their malware more widely.

File transfer protocol (FTP).

Used to store or retrieve files, FTP is another commonly used Application Layer Protocol. It has been developed to allow the transfer of files between a client and a server. An FTP client is an application running on a computer and used to extract files from a server running the FTP daemon (FTPd). To transfer the files correctly, the FTP protocol requires that two connections be established between the client and the server; one connection for the commands and the reply and another for the transfer of the files.

The client establishes the first connection to the server on TCP port 21, this connection is used controlling traffic and consists of client commands and server responses. The client establishes the second connection to the server via TCP port 20, this connection is for the same transfer of files and is established at each file transfer. File transfer can be done in one of two directions, the client can download a file from the server or to the server.

The fact that FTP is used by default without encryption on the server, means that if a hacker gets on the network between the user and the server (main in the middle attack), he can see the password. The passwords are not encrypted. It is the same principle as when connecting to a website with Hypertext Transfer Protocol (HTTP). To secure a connection to a website, it is important to must use the Hypertext Transfer Protocol Secure (HTTPS). In the same way, there is a secure protocol with

FTP, it is the SFTP (SSH File Transfer Protocol). This establishes an encrypted connection between the FTP client and the FTP server. The principle is the same regarding the operation of the FTP protocol, it is simply that a layer of security is added through SSH (secure shell). But there is a small drawback of an SFTP connection is that the connection time will be a little longer because of the encryption. By construction the FTP protocol suffers from some shortcomings in terms of SSI:

It allows the notion of anonymous logon; the default setting allows the user "anonymous", with any password, to connect to the service. · The password of the users circulates in clear on the network.

FTP Protocol Vulnerabilities

FTP Bounce Attack: The principle of this attack is to perform malicious actions through a vulnerable FTP server; seen from the target, it is the FTP server that leads the attack and not the attacker machine. the attacker will use a vulnerable FTP server to send a falsified email. The process is simple, attackers connect to the vulnerable FTP server and places a command file in a Read / Write accessible publication tree, they then reconnects to the server and issues a PORT command; to allow them to instruct the server to open the data port 25 on the address of the target server (the server is asked to log on to port 25, which is the port of messaging, on target.com). If the server executes, attackers enter the command "GET filedfile.txt", which results in sending the contents of the file previously deposited on the TCP connection defined by the PORT command. Since the data file contains valid SMTP commands, the victim of this attack accepts the message. As seen from the victim, the FTP server emitted a valid e-mail appearing to come from the ftp user.

Passive Aggressive Attack

can also be disastrous: Passive cyberattacks use non-disruptive methods and are virtually invisible to detect so that the attacker goes unnoticed. The goal is to collect data without being detected.

SCADA may also be vulnerable to

Stuxnet Attacks

Stuxnet, is the computer worm that attacks SCADA systems. A worm computer can infect and paralyze a whole system of control-command. Thus, SCADA software can be contaminated by a USB storage device (e.g. hard disk, key), the infected SCADA software can in turn contaminate the controllers with which it is connected, which in turn disrupts the functioning of the production system. The consequences of an infected production system can be disastrous, this is especially true in sensitive sectors such as nuclear.

Their effect is the destruction of Program Processing Systems, but also of course the destruction of IT infrastructures, such as magnetic storage or hard disks. But this attack is not much different from the Flame or Duqu Attacks.

Flame or Duqu Attacks

Like Stuxnet, the Flame or Duqu Attacks are likely to target the ICS, just like the Injection Attacks, whose objective is to deflect the industrial system from its normal behavior. The flame indicates that it is designed primarily to spy on infected computer users and steal data, including documents, recorded conversations and keystrokes. It also opens a backdoor for infected systems to allow attackers to modify the toolbox and add new features. The malware, which is twenty megabytes when all of its modules are installed, contains several libraries, SQLite3 databases, different levels of encryption, some of which are strong, and others weaker and twenty plugins that can be exchanged according to various features. It even contains code that is written in the LUA (free scripting language) Programming Language, a rare choice for malware.

Another disastrous attack against critical infrastructures is Active Directory also known as DNA Attacks.

DNA Attacks

Active directory infrastructure remains the hotspot and gateway to cyberattacks. It is however the source of numerous attacks against companies, institutions, and States sites. Active Directory is the mainstay of enterprise computing, its directory infrastructure has the function of managing the identification and authentication of a network for stations under Windows. It plays a central role in access to corporate resources and control of the Information System (IS). From printers, scanners, accounts and user groups, to email and unified communications services, Active Directory is the "custodian" of the information system. Thus, in the era of multiple, complex cyberattacks and as companies are digitizing, internationalize, not to mention the development of "shadow IT", the security of Active Directory must become one of the daily concerns of CIOs, and CISOs (Chief information security officer) and by extension of their Directorate General: and among its weaknesses, the weakest of the AD: the lack of training and investment. The AD is their gateway, hackers just have to find the key to enter the system and test it. Through its hacking action, hackers gain access to data after penetrating AD, they also get access to the emails, messaging, mobile, CEO desktop devices, and other decision-making functions that hold the confidential information of the victim; resulting in ransomware, data exfiltration, industrial spying, critical system control or production processes, and exploit every single flaw while going through the Active Directory. The attacker opens a boulevard to carry out his criminal act, and as we all know that AD is a path to other horizons because of its global and central structure, the hacker would be able to access the networks of partners, customers, and suppliers of all the victims that are interconnected to the Information System (IS) of the attacked infrastructures and into which, the attacker gained access.

There are two main types of attack on the AD:

- The "Golden Ticket" offers access to the Grail of the hacker who creates an ID card making him pass for an AD administrator. Thus, it opens access to all the AD infrastructure of its victim and its ecosystem.
- The "PassThe2Hash": allows the attacker to steal codes and identification secrets (password, etc.) to impersonate a user who arrives in the morning at the office, typing his password, with absolutely no doubt that he just opened and offering access to his PC to the hacker.

These two attacks are gathered under the banner of what is called "Credential Thefts". It is important to remember, AD is natively perfectly secure. It is a very powerful "engine" just like

Formula 1 car has one. But it cannot be precisely regulated by any "mechanic". Those in charge must be trained, which is unfortunately not always the case.

Therefore, AD needs to be secured:

- Going beyond the obvious: Checking administrator accounts is not enough. If AD is a global system, monitoring and setting up countermeasures to detect, isolate, and remediate an attack on the AD must be surgical. The AD requires constant attention to ensure compliance with established security rules, and preserve the security of access rights, thus confidential data
- Avoiding the trap of the "shadow admin" (Hecht and Lazarovitz, 2018) (network accounts that have sensitive privileges and are usually ignored because they are not part of a privileged Active Directory group). It is crucial to establish strong safety barriers. From experience, the model of security followed in business is sometimes quite permissive (a new employee arrives and has rights on the AD that do not have to be).

Nowadays, external service providers are commissioned to install the servers and retain some important permissions on them. This is the famous "shadow administration" that creates the flaw and may compromise Active Directory because it is through this provider that the hacker could go back to the Active Directory. Thus, defining a reliable security model of AD is necessary and isolating sensitive resources, providing the right rights to the right people. Once these barriers are in place, ensure they are sustainable over time, as AD is constantly evolving.

- Mastering the administration populations. By snowball effect, it is necessary to diagnose administrative privileges granted (people, service providers, business, professional and personal applications). Without this, it's certainly given a great responsibility to these administrators who only increases the risk, the attack surface on the AD infrastructure and endangers the IS.

- Educating the internal and explaining the rules. Training in security rules, and securing the Active Directory infrastructure is essential. stating them clearly, explaining why some have restricted rights and others have wider rights. Crumple some ego will not jeopardize the IS, crumple the Active Directory on the other hand can. The rights need to be rationalized.
- Avoiding responding to every cyber security marketing as the cybersecurity industries are ready to sell what they called the "Latest Detection Arsenal". If this is a must, it is not enough. Above all, it is useless not to secure the Active Directory infrastructure. Better to reinforce its security policy, and access/privileges rather than to multiply the products. By strengthening the brick on which the entire information system rests, the IS should already be equipped to effectively anticipate cyberattacks.

-

SOCIAL ENGINEERING ATTACKS

Common Social Engineering Attacks:

Spear Phishing

Like e-mails used in traditional phishing campaigns, targeted phishing messages appear to come from an approved source. If the former gives the impression of coming from a reputable company, website or website with many members, such as Amazon or PayPal, the apparent source of the latter will probably be someone in the recipient company.

The success of targeted phishing depends on three factors:

- The apparent source must present itself as a known and approved person
- Certain information contained in the message must support this validity
- the request of the sender must give an impression of a logic-based.

Most phishing attacks are large. An attacker can send e-mails to hundreds or thousands of people claiming to have an impressive video, an important document or a billing dispute. But sometimes, phishing attacks are targeted based on something the attacker already knows about the person. This is called "harpooning".

Baiting Techniques

In baiting, an attacker prominently leaves an infected device, for example, a USB key. When a person finds it and uses it, it unknowingly loads the malicious program onto its computer.

Data leakage

The priority in data protection is to identify and classify information: public, internal, confidential, and secret. The term "Eyes only" is a code sometimes used to classify "critical" information. The limited visibility offered by current tools to identify targeted data poses a major problem for both IT and business teams. The good questions need to be asked; where are the critical data? With which life cycle? (knowing that data can be critical at a time T and no longer be at T + n).

A cyberattack directly harms the brand image of the affected company. It deprives the company of its usual operation, its essential data for its survival, it also reveals its failure in terms of data security and undermines the trust of customers.

From the hijacking of corporate infrastructures to generate cryptocurrency to the piracy of connected objects through the automation of ransomware, new cyberattacks are known to be difficult to detect.

THE IMMINENT AND NON-NEGLIGIBLE ATTACKS.

Electromagnetic Pulsed:
Targeted Attack.

Indeed, attacks aimed at destabilizing industrial infrastructures such as nuclear plants, aviation or energy are increasing; China and Russia prepare for a "Blackout War" with ultra-powerful electromagnetic pulse bombs (Pry, 2017). Russia has developed powerful high-altitude nuclear bombs that can produce super-electromagnetic pulsed (EMP) waves capable of blasting critical electronic infrastructures, according to Pry (2017a), from the Commission to Assess the Threat to the United States from EMP Attack. They can rightly regard the Electromagnetic Pulse Nuclear Attack as a weapon that can seriously damage the United States by hitting its technological Achilles heel, without having to confront the US military. The report shows how foreign players could launch EMP Attacks virtually anywhere in the world including in Europe and the UK. Such an event could paralyze a State economies and their armed forces. It is a type of nuclear bomb that explodes much higher in the atmosphere to destroy the electronic networks of any enemy State. These EMPs can be emitted by the blast of a nuclear weapon, from portable devices such as High Power Microwave Weapons (HPMW). These powerful pulses - when interacting with the Earth's magnetic field - can damage electronic and electrical equipment such as computers, cell phones, transformers and transmission lines, as well as critical communications infrastructure. Even worse, the design of the power grid means that damage to some critical substations could cause cascading failures throughout the whole State, victim of the attack. And the consequences would be catastrophic for electricity, telecommunications, transportation, gasoline, gas, or water

The EMP has the effect of neutralizing the electrical networks (Pry, 2017b), in addition to the fallout and gamma rays that result from its explosion. The "super electromagnetic pulse weapons", as Russia calls them, are nuclear weapons specifically designed to generate an extraordinarily powerful E1 EMP field. Super-EMP warheads are designed to produce gamma rays, which generate the E1 EMP effect, not a big explosion, and usually have very low explosive efficiencies, only 1-10 kilotons.

ATTACKS AIMED
AT ALTERING
INFORMATION & PROCESSES

Hashing is a powerful tool that can guarantee data integrity. This cryptographic algorithm makes it possible to convert a file or data into a short series of numbers called "hash" in its new SHA-3 or "message synthesis". Made correctly, the latter is unique and specific to the hashed information, the least modification of the information will therefore create a completely different synthesis. A comparison of the syntheses using a Secure Hash Algorithm (SHA-3) hash algorithm will allow any alteration done to be detected immediately.

While confidentiality and availability are two pillars of cybersecurity, data integrity is also important because it ensures the accuracy of data used in transactions and business processes: Data theft can be difficult to avoid or even detect. It is not uncommon for a cyberattack to remain undetected for several months, and the victim will often be aware of the piracy and its extent only at the time of its discovery sometime by a third party. Detecting a leak or data corruption is sometimes even more difficult. If the format of this information has not been modified, their modification will be even more difficult to identify than a theft, although their value has been severely impacted.

However, it should be emphasized that it is not only the data that can be altered but also the process itself. Several attacks can be made for this:

- **Denial of Service**: Denial of Service (DoS) occurs when an attacker disables or alters a network, system, or service to deny the intended service to normal users. Denial of service attacks causes the system to fail or slow down to the point of rendering it unusable. Denial of service can simply consist of deleting or altering information. In most cases, the attack comes down to running a hacker program or script. It is, for this reason, that Denial of Service Attacks are the most feared.

The DoS Attack is the most common form of attack and also the most difficult to eliminate. In the hacker community, this type of attack is even considered trivial and is not popular, because its execution requires little effort. However, the ease of implementation of DoS Attacks and their potentially very serious damage is receiving the attention of security administrators.

DoS Attacks can take many forms. They prevent the use of a service by authorized persons by exhausting the resources of the system. Here are some examples of the most common DoS threats:

Ping fatak --- Flood SYN -------- DDoS -------- Smurf

- Worms, viruses, and Trojans: Malware can be installed on a host computer to damage or corrupt a system, reproduce, or prevent access to networks, systems, or services. These programs are usually called worms, viruses and trojans.
- External attackers can use Internet tools, such as the nslookup and whois, to easily discover the IP addresses assigned to a given company or entity. Once these IP addresses are known, the attacker can ping publicly available addresses to determine which ones are active. To automate this step, the attacker can use a scanning tool like fping or gping, which always sends ping requests to a range of addresses or all addresses in a

subnet. This approach is similar to using a phone book and calling all numbers to find out who is responding.

- **Access Attacks**: Access Attacks exploit known vulnerabilities in Authentication Services, FTP Services, and Web Services to access Web accounts, confidential databases, or other sensitive information.
- **Password Attacks**: Password attacks can be done using a packet analyser to glean accounts and user passwords transmitted in clear. Password attacks typically relate to repeated login attempts to a shared resource, such as a server or router, to identify a user account, password, or both. These repeated attempts are called dictionary attacks or force attacks.
- **Trust Exploitation**: An attack by exploiting trust is intended to compromise a trusted host and then use it to launch attacks on other hosts on the network. In an enterprise network, if a host is protected by a firewall (internal host), but is accessible from a trusted host on the other side of the firewall (external host), the internal host can be attacked through the external host.
- Port Forwarding: Port forwarding is a Trust Exploiting Attack that uses a compromised host to pass traffic through a firewall that would normally be blocked.
- **Man in the Middle Attack**: A Man-in-the-Middle (MIM) Attack is led by a hacker who arranges himself between two legitimate hosts. This attacker can allow normal transactions between the two hosts and only manipulate their conversation from time to time. The reply is transferred through the IPsec protocol suite which makes it vulnerable to such types of threats causing severe damage to the network. The intruders attempt and get success in keeping themselves in between the two nodes or attempt to be the network between the server and the client.
- **Recognition Attacks**: Recognition Attacks can have

the following forms:

Internet Information Requests
Ping Scans ----- Port Scans ------ Packet Analysers
External attackers can use Internet tools, such as the nslookup and whois utilities, to easily discover the IP addresses assigned to a given company or entity. Once these IP addresses are known, the attacker can ping publicly available addresses to determine which ones are active. To automate this step, the attacker can use a scanning tool like fping or gping, which always sends ping requests to a range of addresses or all addresses in a subnet. This approach is similar to using a phone book and calling all numbers to find out who is responding.

Recon-type Attacks

Recon-type Attacks look for weaknesses or vulnerabilities in network defenses. When vulnerabilities are found, they are not directly exploited by the recon attack, but the information inherent to these vulnerabilities is reported to the attackers to enable them to better organize future attacks, and specifically target these vulnerabilities. A well-prepared attacker will be looking for as much information as possible about the infrastructure he wants to attack, rather than launching blind attacks:

- **Malware Attacks**: A worm executes code and installs copies of itself in

the memory of the infected computer, which subsequently infects other hosts.

OTHER ATTACKS

Attack by DHCP
Threats that could be initiated include DHCP Starvation Attack and Rogue Server Attack. The possible countermeasures include the elimination of all default ports in VLAN

ARP Poisoning Attack
There are several tools available from Net for ARP; man-in-the-middle and Ettercap. The possible measures for such type of threat include Dynamic ARP Inspection (DAI).

Spoofing Attacks
Can be categorized into two types MAC Spoofing and IP Spoofing. Some of the countermeasures include IP source guard, clear up source guard, and building the layers including port security, DHCP snooping, DAI, and IPSG.

Sniffing Attack.
This is a threat that can be used by intruders for entering the network and stealing the sensitive and personal information of the users. The goal of the intruders is to steal the credentials of the users and use them for personal unauthorized attempts.

Application Layer Attack:
Application Layer Attack like Buffer Overflow, CGI Attack, and various type of malicious codes that attacks the seventh layer

i.e. Application Layer of the ISO/OSI model is possible and severe threats to the network.

Flooding Attack and Rouge Devices

These are some of the attacks and security threats that are considered for the established network.

Ransomware

The ransomware or WannaCry consists in extorting the organization's sensitive data; the technics consist of blackmailing by claiming huge sums of money. Ransomware is a very common method of hijacking an organization's data and reselling them to the same organization for an excessive amount of money pretending to release them once the money has been received. The method is well known and can include blocking the company network system and preventing them from accessing their data. it consists of injecting malicious computer software and holding the data hostage by encrypting them and saving them into a USB key and to trade back to the victim in exchange for a ransom.

This system of infiltration is well developed in the form of a worm through a downloaded file, this process gives the hacker the ability to infect a file and send it to its potential victims as an email with a malicious link which, once opened, can read and save all the files of the victim on a USB key connected to the end machine under its control. The BYOD will be a boon for hackers to perfect their ransomware techniques by targeting the organization behind the BYOD platform via an employee's machine outside the corporate firewall security. Ransomware can also be sent to its victim during an instant conversation or installed on a public computer; ransomware is an intelligent virus that can read and record promptly. .

IDENTIFYING
VULNERABILITY

To be able to design a well-protected network or system, you will have to put yourself into the "hacker's mind", that is to say ask yourself the following question: how would you proceed to attack a network or a system? All these counter-attacks measures identified above are quite effective, but they are even more so when professionals who perform these measures think just like hackers/attackers do before executing an attack. Thinking like attackers means being able to imagine cyberattacks scenarios that can be put in place to break into your organization's system, and how would they do it. Do not question yourself when, because it's imminent. If you still have a chance of the "when" question, then the attack is about to occur and fortunately, you have a little chance to avoid it or be ready to encounter it. An attack gets effective as soon as a vulnerability of the target is found, which means that the hackers will first look for the vulnerability of the system they are about to break into, hence the importance and implementation of the vulnerability assessment as a protective fog. The vulnerability assessment makes it possible to systematically visualize the security weakness in the information system. It assessed whether the system is sustainable to any known vulnerabilities and assigns the security level to those flaws, then recommends the necessary fix. It is a process of identifying, quantifying and prioritizing vulnerabilities in a system; this process is known as penetration testing or Pen Test. And because this is exactly how the attacker will proceed when preparing an attack, your organization needs to proceed just like that to find if any hole is found and close it before the attacker finds it.

Vulnerability Assessment

Vulnerability assessment can be performed by cataloguing assets and capabilities (resources) in a system to assign a quantifiable value and level of importance to those resources, penetration testers identify potential vulnerabilities or threats to each resource and applied resources (tools) to mitigate or eliminate the most serious vulnerabilities for the most valuable resources first. Some steps need to be taken when assessing vulnerability; security analysis tests, security health of applications, servers, or other systems by scanning them using automatic tools available on the market (OWASP, Xray, Zmap, SimplyEmail, John the Ripper, Hydra, Wireshark, Hashcat and more) and this security scanning process consists of testing, analyzing, assessing, and remediating. The first step is **Vulnerabilities Identification**: the objective of this step is to draft a comprehensive list of all applications security vulnerabilities by the means of scanning, the second step is **Vulnerability Analysis, this** step objective is to help identify the source and the routed cause of vulnerabilities, which means that if the cause of the vulnerability is not clearly identified and eliminated, there will be consequences even after removing some parts of vulnerability. The third step is the **Risk Assessment** which the objective is to prioritize vulnerabilities by assigning the quantifiable value that comes under risk assessment, and the fourth and last step is the **Remediation**, the objective of remediation is the closing of security gaps. This is typically a joint effort between the security staff, the development, and the operation team who determine the most effective part for the remediation and mitigation of each vulnerability. It can include an introduction of new security procedures, implementation of new security measures and introduction to staff of new and latest security tools, and can also include the addition of all operational packages and patches, and the development and implementation of a batch vulnerability which can lead to XML External Entity Injection (XXE) vulnerability.

The vulnerability assessment is NOT a one-off task activity for any organization running SCADA system; this needs to be regularly carried out at least once every month, the vulnerability assessment will provide a way to detect and eliminate security issues by ranking vulnerabilities before the bad guys take control of them and exploit their vulnerability. Scanning the operating systems, application software and the network would help to identify occurrences of vulnerabilities and detect inappropriate software design and insecure authentication, helps in identifying threats and weaknesses earlier before attackers do, and takes remediation actions to close any gaps within the infrastructure; this assessment (scanning) is one of the recommended steps before doing any Penetration Testing to identify flaws in the system; It is carried out by professionals within the IT environment that have good knowledge and programming skills. Pen testers should go through all the steps including those for gathering information included in the organization legal documentation. They also will need to know about the scope assessment which regulated the organization policy in which the penetration testing is taking place, before going through the information assessment to gather as much information they need to carry out the test. These steps above are same steps that hackers used to break into any organization system that they targeted.

Professionals need to check in the Legal Documentation held by the company while preparing for pen testing, they need to ensure that, they understand what Scope Assessment means and what do they need it for, and if you are working as a consultant to this particular company, please ensure you have the permission. Some time, you can find your tasks into the

Scope Assessment document, which you should receive from the company where your test is taking place. Then jump to:

- Information Assessment; to gather as much as information you need, the fourth step will be Scanning for holes or vulnerabilities; this is called Vulnerability Assessment as described above.

After these steps, the system is ready to be tested, now match the results and opt-in for secure Pen-Testing.

The next stage will be:

- Gaining Access: search whatever more holes may be opened and go deeper into the system as far as you can go and gain privileges; this is called Privilege Escalation which consists of breaking into the "no-privilege zone" and navigating to gain more access.

Then jump to:

- Report Generation: extract any information from the system to improve decision-making,

before getting within:

- Patch Assistance step to secure patches, fix bugs if any and apply updates, and make an evaluation

- Evaluation step is to ensure the system is fit to work securely; this is called "Revalidation"

There is in cybersecurity, a logic that must be followed by decision-makers, when It comes to protecting Information Systems, it is necessary to get yourself into the mind of the hacker because you could not protect a system if you do not know against whom to protect It. You should know how hackers operate to know how to counter an imminent attack. And at this point, gathering information is certainly the starting point of a possible attack. Gathering information may include pinging the website of the target, phone number, IP address, location, users and many more; The footprinting lets the attackers know the security posture of the targeted organization and allows them to draw a map or outline the targeted organization's network infrastructure to know about the actual environment that they are going to break into. To achieve their goals, the attackers use social engineering to map the attack surface with continuous security monitoring which could lead to a potential vulnerability or misconfiguration and could be exploited by a threat actor

Pen testing your network or your organization's Information System by simulating an Attack Surface Mapping (ASM), also known as Attack Surface Monitoring, Managing, and Analysing, provides continuous monitoring of the changing attack surface. Specifically, it detects assets that contain, transmit, or process your data while identifying vulnerabilities as they arise. It informs you about the components of your attack surface, where are the attack vectors and exposures, and how to effectively protect your organization against cyberattacks.

Pen testing helps your organization to build a counterattack and eliminate the eventual risks and threats, knowing that, you can't remediate risks that you aren't aware of, and security strategies become meaningless if they aren't risk-based. So, this proactive method of cyber security helps CISOs and security leaders visualize, understand, and analyze their changing threat landscape. Implementing a continuous security monitoring process will empower you to make more informed cybersecurity decisions and improve productivity.

SYSTEM
PROTECTION

After all that is known about the SCADA system, its operation and its exposure to risks, but also the importance of critical infrastructures, it is more than necessary to develop a real strategy that combines new technologies to cope with cyber risk:

Main Applications of Artificial Intelligence in Cyber Security

Cyber Security is the set of technical, organizational, legal and human means (National Initiative for Cybersecurity Education Working Group, 2018) necessary, to put in place tools capable to prevent the unauthorized use, misuse, modification or misuse of information systems. It assures the self-independence and the safety of the information system by posing itself as a means of information system management. Computer systems' risk can be understood in a fairly simple way: what will happen if all the electronics of the company have been cut off, from computers to production, via the smartphones of the managers? Most companies will be totally paralyzed and some of them will not survive. All companies are currently working on digital projects (Global Industry 4.0 Survey, 2016), on redesigning their information system. However, if a problem occurs in the monitoring and management of these projects, they can become a major risk for the company and face cyber threats. Today's antivirus and firewall-based solutions only stop the threats they face: viruses from an already-signed signature or malware from a snippet of lines of code that are characteristic of it. Beyond that, cyber hackers who design sophisticated and tailored attacks according to the profile of their targets - the famous APT (advanced persistent threat) act in the networks in a manner virtually undetectable.

Unlike antivirus or firewalls, cybersecurity based on learning algorithms could neutralize unknown cyberattacks (deepinstinct, 2018). The exfiltration of sensitive data, bank card theft or the piracy of movies and messaging and so on. So many security breaches that have hit the headlines in recent years could have been avoided if the hacked facilities had resorted to cybersecurity doped with Artificial Intelligence (AI) and could have stopped sophisticated cyberattacks and those exploiting vulnerabilities discovered by hackers, but still unknown to the computer community. Indeed, Artificial Intelligence as it is used is based on the use of neural networks and probabilistic or deterministic algorithms (Xiang et al, 2018). These feed on data, allowing the processing of a large volume of information. AI is today a major technological advance that promises to disrupt in the coming years a large number of markets (KPMG, 2018). These upheavals are already a reality in sectors such as finance, entertainment, transportation or customer support services. But the use of AI has also imposed itself in another area: that of Cyber Security. Because one of its main assets is its ability to handle very large amounts of complex data and to perform massively repetitive tasks in record time (DHL Trend Research, 2018), without human intervention: a decisive advantage for cybersecurity operations. In Cyber Security, AI technologies (as a tool) can improve cyberthreat intelligence and prediction and enhance protection against such threats (Thales, 2017). They can also accelerate attack detection and response times while reducing the need for human experts in cybersecurity. AI can learn from security analysts and improve its performance over time, saving time and making better decisions. These "smart cybersecurity" capabilities are of utmost importance as cyberattacks continue to grow in volume and complexity. Analytics and Big Data are key drivers for AI, enabling the processing and analysis of large amounts of data; parsing, filtering and visualization are done in real-time. The adoption of advanced analytics is also an essential step toward becoming an information-oriented organization. The use of AI technologies can improve cybersecurity capabilities and manage cyber risks more efficiently and effectively (Deloitte, 2018).

Traditional approaches to managing network security rely primarily on manual processes, and pre-established strategies for identifying and blocking attacks are no longer able to keep pace with the emergence of new threats. Because handling an ever-increasing volume of threat indicators is an intensive and time-consuming process for security teams. This is where AI brings considerable added value. It saves time, correlates more data, makes faster, more consistent decisions, reduces the risk of human error, and predicts threat evolution while improving the business security posture, and It is sad to see that unfortunately, many companies, do not have the necessary staffing and security expertise (Lacey and James, 2010). AI can automate security processes and save time, which can be spent on more strategic tasks by IT teams. Indeed, the AI can perform functions that normally require the intervention of a qualified security analyst, to analyse huge amounts of security data (Financial Stability Board, 2017) and act automatically to improve the overall level of security. Properly implemented, the AI can perform correlation, analysis and scoring tasks for these companies while constantly improving thanks to Machine Learning (Financial Stability Board, 2017) and AI Deep Learning, further guaranteeing their cyber-vigilance. In addition, AI can automate incident resolution by minimizing business disruption.

Security policies based only on signature databases can quickly become obsolete and out of date. AI provides new, intelligent layers of protection that can detect and counter new generation malware much faster and more efficiently than older approaches. Properly configured, the AI provides predictive protection that anticipates future threats without the need for signature databases, cloud connectivity, and more. It can examine several hundreds of thousands of components of a given file to determine almost instantly its level of danger. Artificial Intelligence is a valuable ally for security teams. But its impact is double-edged. As it is also increasingly used by cybercriminals, to improve their targeting, expand the impact of their attacks and accelerate the speed with which they create new malware more effective (Brundage *et al*):

1. To be fully effective and maintain the advantage in all circumstances, an Artificial Intelligence solution applied to cybersecurity must be able to automate both prevention, detection and response to attacks, and this is done 24hours and 7days.
2. Preventing through predictive coverage. The delay between discovering malware and taking into account signatures and patterns of malicious behavior remains a major challenge for all security teams. Artificial Intelligence must be able to predict emerging threats several months before their appearance.
3. Shorten the detection times. By relying on the static and dynamic analysis capabilities of thousands of malicious indicators continuously, Artificial Intelligence must be able to detect and virtually destroy all-new threats before they can attack the network.
4. Automate protection processes. Collecting and processing huge amounts of data from a variety

of sources is a core capability of Artificial Intelligence, but it must enable it, through powerful Machine Learning and Deep Learning capabilities, to continually improve the effectiveness of its response to threats, and thereby the overall security posture of the company.

Artificial Intelligence technologies are increasingly being used in the fight against threats. Thanks to Machine Learning, which is already well known to researchers, AI makes it possible to approach security differently and better adapted to the evolving context of cybercrime, with more anticipation and reliance on behavioral analyzes. Applications have already come out of the labs, especially via open-source libraries, but new skills are needed. By improving its knowledge and understanding of phenomena by itself, Machine Learning facilitates the detection of an attack even if it does not know its signature; by studying techniques that allow systems to learn for themselves from their own experiences.

Technically speaking, these are algorithms that allow a system to adapt its analyses and behaviours, in response to information coming in the form of empirical and unstructured data from other systems, databases or sensors. Machine learning has already many applications: recognition of images, objects and writing, search engines, help with medical diagnostics and breakdowns, financial and stock market analysis, robotics, semantic analysis of opinion, feeling and consumer behavior for targeted marketing campaigns.

Traditionally, cybersecurity relies on file signatures to identify malware and rules to detect anomalies in network traffic. These methods require knowledge of a large number of factors: malicious files must be known, and have been observed and analysed beforehand. The same is true of rule-based systems: these are based on the experience of what might be malicious activity.

In a context of increasing cyberattacks linked to the growing volume of data and equipment to be monitored, cybersecurity techniques are evolving to cope with the limitations of filter, rule and signature detection capabilities. In this confluence of events, Machine Learning is a good option to meet the need for automation to detect unknown threats, especially in the oil sector. More broadly, the digitization of factories, public transport, banks and automobiles are also concerned. From the point of view of Information Systems, the digital transformation of companies results in systems that are increasingly open and heterogeneous in terms of infrastructure, nature of applications or data. This complex environment is associated with growing problems around the access of various populations of users to information. current security solutions are showing their limits in cybersecurity: the databases of signatures (malware detection and filtering rules) are always behind on the techniques of hacking; security systems and applications are not scalable enough to cope with the increase in the phenomenon; the current detection systems are not adapted to highly distributed environments ... and finally, the solutions are passive, non-preventive and depend on human intervention. An attack must be known to recognize it using signatures already observed, before countering it. Thanks to its self-learning abilities, machine learning makes it possible to detect deviant behaviors in advance by analyzing massive amounts of data in multiple formats, relying on behavioral analyzes and improving its knowledge on its own. and his understanding of phenomena. It thus facilitates anticipation by detecting an attack even if the signature is not known. The aim is to strengthen the development of automated methods for analyzing complex and massive data to extract information useful for preventive detection. Like Big Data, it has become clear that the more data flows, the more it increases the need for processing capabilities (processes, analyzes and actions) that only machines can satisfy. The problem with these methods is their reactive nature: attackers find innovative ways to circumvent known rules, and before an expert finds out, it's often too late. In this context, artificial intelligence can bring to cybersecurity a new ability to adapt: it is no longer a question of following specific rules or looking for signatures, but of comparing what is observed with predefined models. from the knowledge acquired in the past, but evolving and less strict than signatures or rules. Where a signature-based approach provides one-to-one threat mapping, data science uses collective learning based on all the threats are seen in the past to proactively identify new threats that have never been seen before. Above all, it is to go beyond the static footprint of a file to look at behavioral specificities. Ransomware, for example, scans the files, identifies the ones it will attack, makes an encrypted copy, then deletes the originals, and sends the encryption key to its operators. Behavioral models can quickly identify such sequences, including for unknown ransomware. And it's all the more important that their operators make sure that they evolve rapidly: it is not uncommon for a decryption tool to be available for such a malware ... at the same time as the diffusion of its new variant. The difference is there, holistic and artificial intelligence-based protection tools look for these sequences of events and report things they do not like, unlike traditional security based on a signature, which merely reports software or pieces of software that have been seen before and are known as malicious.

The other strength of AI is intelligence combined. A computer system consists of different software components, each with its security mechanisms and activity logs, its logs. An analytic system can continuously monitor the set of trends across all systems in the given infrastructure. Artificial Intelligence can build a complete view of the actions each user performs, allowing them to better track malicious actions and eliminate false alarms. These security systems using artificial intelligence are a whole new challenge for attackers: not only must they deceive the security controls, but they must do it intelligently, with finesse and subtlety. Brutal attacks and robot attacks could mean attackers will also have to use artificial intelligence to infiltrate; as a result, CIOs need to understand the limitations and weaknesses of the new systems they deploy. Unfortunately, IT professionals tend to be complacent once a cybersecurity system based on AI is put in place. in place. They somehow suppose that this new system will learn quickly enough to protect itself against all the attacks.

Current artificial Intelligence engines use statistical data to classify trends as malicious or benign. But the adaptability of these engines can also become their weakness. Many systems can detect anomalies initially, but after a while, they learn to accept them as normal behaviors. And precisely, attackers usually hide their activities by observing normal behavior, such as sending data to a server or printer via an HTTPS call. In fact, since the strength of statistical algorithms lies in the recognition of models and schemas, attackers are likely to gradually adapt their behaviors so that they appear normal, or to carry out their actions to induce confusion. The machine has no context on what is normal as a human activity. Therefore, it is possible to add all kinds of strange signals that will have no meaning for a human analyst but will tell the machine that it is facing normal activity. And that, the most advanced attackers already understand it. And it is to notice that the vast majority of the claims received as a result of a computer attack involve a human error in one form or another and they usually come from simple things like phishing, SQL injection, remote access over the Internet, and weak passwords.

Artificial Intelligence provides an additional layer of security which is likely to slow down hackers significantly. Maybe even to the point of diverting them to systems that do not have such protection because they are easier to access. But no system is safe. Attackers' efforts are proportional to the value of their target. And high-level cybercriminals, linked to States, will persist until they succeed in infiltrating and settling permanently. However, for that reason It is important to keep in mind: that security is a process, not a product. Artificial Intelligence affects all aspects of human social life. they interact daily with smart systems that optimize their travel, create favourite playlists or protect their email boxes from unwanted emails. They invisibly serve humans. according to the objective assigns to them; which is to make our lives better. The growing influence of AI on human life and its recent progress in many areas has placed it at the centre of public debate and raises questions about its ability to work for the well-being of users and to take to achieve it. Leading to a broad reflection on the ethical issues related to the development of Artificial Intelligence technologies and more broadly algorithms. Experts, regulators, academics, entrepreneurs and citizens regularly discuss current and potential adverse effects and ways to mitigate them Placed under the necessity of articulating the potential offered by these technologies with respect for social values and norms, these discussions logically drew on the vocabulary of ethics. They have invested the available space between what is made possible by AI and what is allowed by law to discuss what is desirable. Now, ethics is precisely that branch of philosophy that devotes itself exclusively to the study of this space by attempting to distinguish good from evil, the ideal towards which to tend and the paths that distance it from humans.

Moreover, far from purely speculative considerations about the existential threats of AI to humanity, the reflections have crystallized around the algorithms of the "daily": those who organize news feeds, guide the decisions of purchases or determine the sports training programs. Not all users are equal before these algorithms and their bias has real consequences on lives. Every day, in a very opaque way, they affect access to information, culture, employment or credit. Therefore, while it is desirable to develop AI technologies that are consistent with social values and norms, action must be taken now by mobilizing the scientific community, governments, industry, entrepreneurs and civil society organizations. . That's why I recommend that companies managing critical infrastructure tried to propose even modestly, some ways to lay the foundations of an ethical framework for the development of AI and to bring this debate into their management and IT teams:

- In the first place, it is necessary to increase the transparency and auditability of autonomous systems on the one hand, by developing the capacities necessary to observe, understand and audit their functioning and, on the other hand, by investing heavily in research on explicability.
- Secondly, the protection of rights and freedoms must be adapted to the potential abuses associated with the use of machine learning systems. However, it turns out that the current legislation, focused on the protection of the individual, is not in phase with the logic introduced by these systems - that is to say the analysis of a considerable mass of information to identify hidden patterns and behaviors - and their effects on groups of individuals. To bridge this gap, it is necessary to act by creating collective rights over the data.
- At the same time, it must be ensured that organizations deploying and using these systems remain liable to the law for any damage caused by them. While the terms of this liability regime remain to be defined, the Computer and Freedoms Act (1978) and GGPI (2018) already lay down the principles.
- However, the law cannot do everything, among other things because the time of the law is much longer than that of the code. It is therefore essential that the "architects" of the digital society - researchers, engineers and developers - who design and market these technologies take their fair share in this mission by acting responsibly. This implies that they are

fully aware of the possible negative effects of their technologies on society and that they are actively working to limit them.

· Moreover, given the importance of ethical issues for future developments of AI, it is necessary to create a real forum for debate, plural and open to society, so that users can determine democratically what AI they wish for their communities.

· Finally, the politicization of issues related to technology in general and AI in particular is made more necessary every day, given the importance that it takes in human life.

There is a tendency today, through the media coverage of techno and its flagship applications (autonomous vehicles in mind), to reduce AI to machine learning alone or deep learning. However, many other techniques exist (Bayesian statistical methods, decision trees, reasoning from Rule-Based Reasoning; RBR rules). One common point, however: is algorithmic that drives the actions of the machine. But even in this field, different programming languages (Lisp, Prolog, C ++, Scheme ...) co-exist alongside techniques that are also distinct depending on the objective pursued

Artificial Intelligence (AI) is at the center of new technologies and new approaches to cybersecurity (Linden et al., 2019). The protection and enhancement of the tools of these investments in research and development are essential: the sustainability of the global economic model and the valorization of innovations are at stake. Artificial Intelligence is the "flagship" technology of the data economy. His method of deep learning enriched by the capture of data perfectly illustrates it. It manages to detect known and unknown cyberattacks. But the question is not theoretical since, according to some European experts (Enisa, 2018), Artificial Intelligence cyberattacks have already started: "Some of the attacks use methodologies and attack vulnerabilities that are already known; others, the most sophisticated ones, use creative solutions and unknown techniques" (Enisa 2018).

This research has given some details of possible operating modes. But to fully understand the danger of Artificial Intelligence in the hands of cyber-attackers, it is necessary to return to the basics of its operation. One of its essential workings is the machine learning engine. It is equivalent to the learning capacity of human beings but on a much larger scale and speed. At the start of producing an AI, the engineer submits to its Machine Learning engine a lot of information by indicating each time whether the phenomenon to be identified is new or not. As the information is swallowed, the engine of Machine Learning develops very pointed conjunction of statistics which, in fine, allows it to determine alone when the phenomenon sought is manifested. there is not a single case that artificial intelligence cannot treat.

With counter-techniques of artificial intelligence in its possession, an attacker will be able to send malware to attack sites protected by captcha (Completely Automated Public Turing test to tell Computers and Humans Apart). Captchas are those systems where the user is invited to show that he knows how to recognize a fancifully written word, or elements among an image, to prove that he is indeed a human. Once a code succeeds to pretend to be a user, this protection is now cracked and it becomes possible to penetrate previously unattackable services. Artificial intelligence could be used for reconnaissance phases to target information systems, allowing AI to know exactly what known vulnerabilities it will encounter and even exploit them automatically thus greatly facilitating this tedious phase of cyberattack. an AI can also be used to identify what another AI is searching for in the data feeds that allow the attacker to send information to mislead the target's alertness.

Accounts Takeover Attacks (ATAs)

ATAs are an important attack based on the illegal appropriation of data and their confiscation for indiscriminate use by hackers. Implementing enhanced multifactor authentication for both account access and transactions protects the user beyond the connection and assure organizations that any risk activity is secured: push notification, biometrics, unique access code, hardware token, or device verification, all of which are multifactor authentication methods that allow an application to be accessed by individuals. These methods can be very effective in protecting the BYODs (Bring Your Own Device) of employees who work in these vital infrastructures, even so, it is more secure to simply forbid the use of BYOD by employees of nuclear centers for example or within water filtration installations and many others.

Since there is a chance that employees with a corporate phones, used them for private tasks. Therefore, it is a good practice to integrate multi-factor authentication into mobile applications using software already tested. The Software Development Kit (SDK) is used by developers to integrate software on an IOS platform, Android or others for their enhanced authentication.

During the period of Covid 19, the vulnerability of the Bring Your Own Device has increased. To keep the business going, more employees were asked to work from home thru a business continuity policy enabling the employees to communicate with their corporate network to ensure the continuity of activity; this has accelerated the use of BYOD, thus vulnerabilities. BYOD involves the physical transportation of data by the user, which increased the risk of loss and thief of sensitive corporate information and data and increase employee vulnerability. Employees using BYOD are more likely to use the same device for private and professional tasks to access WLAN and to navigate WIFI corporate network, leading increasingly to more vulnerabilities whether or not a firewall is installed. Those employees with professional mobiles may be tempted for installing personal apps while visiting unsecured websites, downloading files for personal use, playing games and receiving and sending photos using social media networks; this can expose them to more vulnerabilities allowing the outsider to hijack corporate database and to infect mobile applications installed for inter-communication between them and their corporate network.

The operation of WLAN is based on several technology gates giving each a specific role through communication channels all different but which come together to form a topology around the WLAN, each of which involves a route that is unique, thus, obeying common rules. All these routes have advantages for improving users' everyday life but also vulnerabilities that are seized by the attackers to lead harmful actions against humans and objects connected together through the scheme of the network. Easy to install, mobility, profitable, and flexible, Wireless LANs are designed with a marginal theoretical difference in the range capabilities of Frequency Hopping Spread Spectrum (FHSS) and Direct Sequence Spread Spectrum (DSSS) systems and operate in license-free bands making their operation and maintenance costs affordable (Khayat 2002).

The inter-connectivity of humans with humans through objects (IoT) or applications (BYOA), machines with machines (Laptops, PCs, Smartphones, PDA...) or smartphones with Users within the critical infrastructure sector can nevertheless reveal vulnerabilities; if they are maliciously used can have consequences disastrous for the daily life of humans.

To protect the confidentiality and integrity of WLAN communication, organizations should ensure that all WLAN components use Information Processing Standards-approved cryptographic algorithms (Frankel S et al. 2006)

Considering that Critical infrastructure organizations should take into consideration the types of data and functionality that are exposed through the deployment and any implementation of the risk profile for all information security risks, how the organization defines and treats risk, plays a key role in choosing the type of security controls the organization should employ

(Insights 2013a) when considering to employ BYOD. However, BYOD is a new way to think about risks. As BYOD introduces risk to the organization, a holistic and methodical approach should be used to define this risk and help to ensure that controls exist to maintain both the security and usability of the devices in the enterprise (Insights 2013b). And the critical infrastructure sector is not spared.

According to the General Data Protection Regulations (GDPR), in particular on its Article 5 (f) states that personal data shall be; "processed in a manner that ensures appropriate security of the personal data, including protection against unauthorised or unlawful processing and accidental loss, destruction or damage, using appropriate technical or organisational measures ((NHS, 2018).

Multi-Factor Authentication (MFA)

MFA can be of little help to BYOD, It is a security system that uses multiple authentication methods, from different categories of credentials (evidence), to verify identity. of the user who wants to connect or make a transaction. It thus makes it possible to verify that the mobile phone has not been compromised and helps the companies to look after the account of their employee when this one is connected in VPN or WIFI.

If the user does not have a network connection but needs to access his device, offline modes can generate a one-time password. This one-time password can also be provided by SMS, voicemail, email or desktop application. A YubiKey token and other hardware tokens can also be used in sensitive environments or for users without access to a mobile device or phone.

Contextual multi-factor authentication works in the background to develop an active and passive evaluation of the user. These may be contextual, behavioral or correlated factors, such as geolocation, the IT environment and the nature of the transaction. It collects user data to establish a typical behavioral profile. If the user's behavior does not match this typical profile, they may require step authentication to apply the appropriate level of security based on the associated risk.

Intrusion Detection Systems (IDS)

IDS is used to identify abnormal or suspicious activity on a given network or target. the intrusion detection technologies used to combine two types of hardware. First, low-level probes that analyze data using behavioral approaches or by recognizing attack signatures.

And then, correlation tools of events are raised by the low-level probes (or SIEM for Security Information and Event Management). Nevertheless, these tools remain imperfect. They have several limitations: the generation of a large number of alerts; the insufficiency of correlation functions, especially in the case of "heterogeneous" alerts; Incomplete and imprecise diagnosis that requires frequent intervention by administrators the problem of false positives, that is to say, the generation of false alarms; or the problem of false negatives, that is, undetected attacks, like "Zero-day" vulnerabilities. In other words, new emerging vulnerabilities: those that have not been published yet.

They have a clear goal: to search and identify new threats in ever-larger volumes of data In the end, these new techniques make it possible both to improve detection techniques (based on behavioral analysis) and to develop new threat detection capabilities.

The growing standardization of these systems and their connection - and hence their openness - to the Internet makes them more vulnerable than ever to cyberattacks.

The fact is that these attacks do not often have financial motivations (according to the survey) and those companies can be state-owed or simply companies classified as critical infrastructures; therefore, they enter into the field of cyber espionage or state cyberterrorism pushing the European Union to establish a permanent council to help enforce targeted restrictive measures (it's the strategy of alliances) aimed at discouraging and countering cyberattacks that pose an external threat to the EU or its member states; this framework allows for the first time the EU to impose sanctions on persons or entities that:

- Are responsible for cyberattacks or cyberattacks attempt
- Provide financial, technical or material support for such attacks
- are involved in any other way in these attacks

But also on persons or entities associated with them. This framework also applies to cyberattacks against third States or international organizations where restrictive measures are deemed necessary to achieve the objectives of the Common Foreign and Security Policy.

User Behavior Analytics (UBA)

UBA is one of the most promising branches of AI-based cybersecurity. It allows knowing finely the functioning of a network or the behavior of a user, to react as quickly as possible in case of an anomaly. Typically, if a large amount of data leaves the network outside normal hours, the AI may issue an alert. Or if the password of a user is hit slower than normal (due to hesitation for example) or from a new computer, it may reveal the theft of security credentials of the real owner.

The new solutions will be able to stop elaborate cyberattacks and those exploiting vulnerabilities discovered by hackers, but still unknown to the IT community. As said above, current antivirus and firewall-based solutions only stop the threats they experience, for example, viruses from a listed signature or malicious software from a snippet of clean lines of code.

cyberattack detection automatic learning algorithms tested to date analyze in real-time the behavior of a network based on a certain number of parameters. This tool is self-configuring for each user connected.

On the other hand, one of the biggest problems with the traditional login mode using an ID and password is that a database of these passwords needs to be maintained. Whether encrypted or not, if a hacker gets their hands on this basis, he will have a possibility to check his assumptions at speeds without any limit other than his material resources. In other words, decrypting a password database is only a matter of time.

With increasing processing speeds, brute force attacks become a real threat. Likewise, other advances, such as password cracking by GPGPU (general-purpose graphics processing unit) technology and rainbow tables, benefit hackers. GPGPU cracking, for example, can produce more than five hundred thousand passwords per second, even on low-end gaming hardware (Phox, 2017).

If "all" artificial intelligence techniques are appropriated by hackers, they can commit cyberattacks by hacking all connected objects, the links between artificial intelligence, the Internet of Things (IoT) and cybersecurity is a real issue on which all IT professionals agree. However, Artificial Intelligence can provide a large-scale response to the piracy of IoT. AI is a real benefit of automation in analysis operations, and sometimes in the manual processing of events, which are now automated, for faster and more efficient processing of a large volume of data. It will reduce The time before the detection of an imminent attack.   AI will be able to target weak signals and detect threats or attacks in progress, including if these threats are new and therefore completely unknown from any existing security solutions.

While using IoT in SCADA improves equipment agility and efficiency through real-time monitoring controls and advanced methods for maintenance controls like secure data transfer, automatic data extraction, and machine idle time collection, having too many more endpoints connected to SCADA networks helps hackers to have more doors to communicate with their victims and will try them all until they find one left open. The Internet of Things (IoT) has kept the attention of IT professionals and the Board of Directors, forgetting the implementation of a real strategy capable of mitigating the risks caused by an attack, this reliance on IoT is now inevitable and their impact on changing attitudes towards confidentiality and security is very high shifting attention has to implementation of risk management strategies to anticipate and deal with eventual attacks against IoT. Organizations that do not want to stay behind jump on these services for better use of the performances of their employees, bringing (unfortunately) with them all the risks related to the instability of such a project. IoT will open more doors for hackers, widening their nuisance radius like a bonus for cybercriminals. And make those devices that will fall into the hands of hackers vulnerable, gain control of the corporate platform, and highjack their database.

CHAPTER 3

- ❖ Security of SCADA Within Critical Infrastructure
- ❖ Business Plan
- ❖ Recovery Plan Or Continuity Of Activity
- ❖ Resilience
- ❖ Ethical Considerations
- ❖ Literature Review
- ❖ Methodology
- ❖ Findings
- ❖ Results
- ❖ Survey Results

SECURING SCADA
TO PROTECT CRITICAL INFRASTRUCTURES

To achieve the required level of protection for industrial and critical networks, security must evolve from simply overlaying technologies to an efficient workflow. An effective security strategy must be able to detect abnormal behavior and block attacks while providing companies with the means to investigate attacks when they occur. The security policy must ensure that any activity is independently logged that is not related to SCADA equipment configuration since it can be hacked by intruders. A repository of the normal behavior of SCADA equipment should define what is allowed, what is prohibited, and what is considered suspicious. Once this is established, the strategy should include automatic notification and prevention of deviations from the repository, to take much more appropriate action against unwanted network exploitation.

In addition to establishing a strategy, it is also essential that the entire corporate IT network is secure to protect SCADA equipment. The attacks of recent years showed that the computing environment, which is generally connected to the Internet, can be a means of access to the operating environment. As such, it is essential to use access restriction mechanisms, such as application control and identity support, as well as firewall, intrusion prevention, antivirus, and emulation threats. A key element of multi-layered defense for SCADA equipment should include threat intelligence, to share and gather intelligence on new threats and emerging threats targeting critical infrastructure. This threat intelligence allows companies to defend their network against cyberthreats before they enter, and to better protect SCADA devices and make them less vulnerable to attack.

Application control and identity support

Application control guarantees the confidentiality and security of the data used and transmitted between the applications, It is a security practice that helps to prevent, restrict or block unauthorized applications from executing wrong code in a way that data are at risk. But to ensure better control of applications, it is necessary to take into account several control elements such as; the completeness and validity checks: to ensure records processing from initiation to completion and that only the valid data is processed, input checks: to ensure data integrity feeds into the application system from upstream sources, forensic checks: to ensure mathematically and scientifically that input and output data are correct, identification: to guarantee unique and irrefutable identification of all users, authentication: this control is to provide a mechanism of an application system authentication, and authorization: this control helps to ensure application system access only to approved users. Application controls ensure adequate coverage and the confidentiality, integrity, and availability of the application and the data associated with it. Application control is also necessary to allow your organization to learn about security policies, and zones to get a complete picture of application usage patterns and traffic, source and destination of traffic, which enables them to make more informed decisions about how to secure applications and identify risky behaviors. While they make these decisions, the application control solution automatically protects the network with whitelisting and blocking capabilities. Wen application controls are correctly implemented, organizations significantly reduce the risks and threats associated with the use of an application as this control can identify any used non-genuine application, prevent it from executing and consequently prevent putting the network or sensitive data at risk. The application control helps use a sort of "comparison table" to distinguish the reliability of applications and classify them by categories between those that are legitimate (whitelisting) and those that must be stopped (blacklisting) from executing. Application control solutions provide visibility into applications, users, and content. This is useful for understanding what data is under the control of your organization, where it is stored, who has access to it, what and where are access points, and the data transmission process. To be able to classify data to help manage risks and for regulatory compliance purposes, these Application controls within the organization are required. Application Control supports these processes and allows organizations to keep tabs on what's going on within their network.

With application control, companies of all sizes can eliminate the risks posed by malicious, illegal, and unauthorized software and network access. It gives organizations a true picture of key areas regarding applications, web traffic, threats, and data patterns. It helps users better understand threats within applications and well understand the key feature of applications and behavioral characteristics.

Firewall

Critical infrastructure protection is the process of securing vital infrastructures, whether physical or virtual, across and outside the network and a firewall is the gatekeeping device that can allow or prevent specific traffic from entering or leaving the network. Installing a firewall will allow the "cross-checking" for any public or unknown listed of harmful websites to prevent them from entering an organization's network, It ensures better privacy and security. A firewall is also able to identify and reject other unwelcome elements of web traffic that an organization do not want to give access to, such as viruses and crypto lockers. It protects against outside cyberattacks by shielding all the organization's devices and networks from malicious or unnecessary network traffic. The firewall will prevent hackers and remote access from accessing non-authorized valuable data and provide better security and network monitoring features.

Intrusion prevention

An intrusion prevention system (IPS) is an automated network security device used to monitor and respond to potential threats. IPS systems can determine the presence of threats by analyzing network traffic. There are two different IPS detection methods: One is Signature-based detection which works by analyzing network data and traffic and looking for specific patterns associated with intrusion attempts. This is similar to traditional virus protection systems based on virus definitions. Signature-based intrusion detection is based on intrusion signatures or patterns. The main disadvantage of this detection method is the slowness of updates. The frequency and speed of signature updates is an important factors to consider when choosing a provider. The other one is Anomaly-based detection; It provides better protection against zero-day attacks, those that occur before detection signatures have had a chance to update. The process looks for anomalies rather than trying to recognize known intrusion patterns. For example, this would trigger if someone tried to access a system with the wrong password multiple times in a row, a common sign of a brute force attack.

Antivirus

Security is more about layers than isolated defense points. Protecting the outer layer of your network organization and the endpoints can be critical. Endpoint protection starts with a powerful antivirus and malware detection and prevention software. Antivirus can scan files while copying, opening or saving. When real-time protection finds a virus in a file, it stops the current operation and does not allow the virus to self-activate. Antivirus will scan and detect unwanted executable applications or DLL libraries in the system which may contain spyware or/and adware, and this is done by scanning system registries for suspicious entries, temporary internet files, and cookies, and potentially harmful items or infections will be cleaned up or quarantined. Incoming and outgoing e-mails will also be checked using plug-ins designed for e-mail programs like E-mail Scanner: monitoring e-mails, designed for applications supporting SMTP/POP3 protocols.

Emulation threats

"Know your enemy as well as yourself" is an oft-quoted maxim in computer security circles. It seems that businesses face new adversaries daily, launching attacks, disrupting their operations and stealthily siphoning off confidential data, thanks to a staggering amount of malware. All of this contributes to making "knowing the enemy" a difficult task. Cybercrime has become big business, and just like in any other industry, criminals are looking to increase their revenue and grow their market share. Their attacks target thousands, of businesses to increase their chances of success. Stealth malware is the most commonly used attack technique: they are designed to be undetected. Observing, emulating, sharing, and defending is known as threat emulation. Emulation allows you to look inside suspicious files that arrive in the gateway, and inspect their content in a virtualized quarantine area called a sandbox. Files are opened there and monitored for unusual behavior in real-time, such as attempts to make abnormal registry changes or unauthorized network connections. When behavior is deemed suspicious or malicious, the file is blocked and quarantined, preventing any infection from reaching the network and causing damage.

BUSINESS
CONTINUITY PLAN

Business continuity systems are often seen by organizations as mere checklists and worklists instructions to use only in unlikely situations, far from the way they do their normal business (Advisera, 2016).

According to Info Entrepreneurs, "failure to plan could be disastrous, and carefully thought-out business continuity plan will make coping in a crisis easier and enable to minimise disruption to the business and its customers" (2019). Poorly coordinated communication from an organization facing a disaster due to a cyberattack can make a lasting contribution to degrading its image. "Preparedness is essential in securing the right to life with dignity" (World Health Organization, 2007)

Disasters due to cyberattacks or natural disasters exert considerable development pressure. and significantly reduce the chances of achieving the Development Goals of an organization. The questions should always be what will happen if your organization suffered a disaster that would prevent it from working properly, would the company be able to continue operating while implementing a defence to limit and control the impact to preserve its reputation, are there any tools do the company expect to use to mitigate risks, is there any document that includes the scope and the governance of their Business Continuity Management System (BCMS), such as a
~}business continuity policy to build a consistent business

continuity strategy. Business continuity strategy should be based on the limitation of the operational impact and the ability to preserve the reputation of the company; which means that, If a problem arises, the company must be able to limit the operational impact by continuing to run and preserve its reputation by using the standards or policy tools. In other words, impact management, and reputation protection are among others, two major pillars of Business Continuity Management (BCM) for any serious organization running a private or State-owned critical infrastructure. Serious disruptions are not always the result of major disasters that directly affect critical infrastructures, for example, the company may be evacuated as a result of an attack by an explosion elsewhere on the industrial site or in the immediate vicinity. Business continuity management is often devolved to the IT(Information Technology) Security department. However, there are more IT risks than security risks and the IT risk function must, therefore, cover all aspects of IT. Some of the IT trends that can affect BCM include Bring Your Own Device (BYOD) and cloud-related applications (Apps) as the major challenge of a BYOD policy lies in the universality of authentication, users do not want to remember many passwords. Each device has password protection capabilities, but unless the user oversees the passwords, many will take the easy way out of removing this basic security check. These IT trends make the determination and delineation of roles and responsibilities even more important. Management must redouble its attention to the independence and invisible attributions of all assets. Nor should they underestimate the cultural changes engendered by trends. BYOD devices such as Android phones, tablets, iPhones, iPads, and more have a catalog of new applications, including those that improve productivity (Cisco, 2015). However, applications may include malicious components designed to introduce viruses or steal data (Google, 2017). While application catalogs are based on different evaluation criteria, it is risky to assume that all applications are safe for all business environments. Even if a client device does not have direct access to the company's file servers or other resources, there is nothing to prevent the application from launching denial of service attacks, ransomware, or other malicious behaviors.

Many companies managing critical infrastructures have deployed security solutions such as VPNs but these often reject the devices BYOD identifying them as lack of software and hardware compatibility, and not supported by Token, so it is necessary to ensure that flows rely on HyperText Transfer Protocol (HTTP) to avoid any operating problem. For this reason, the adoption of an open and non-binding protocol of the Hyper-Text Transfer Protocol Secure (HTTPS) type must be used. Encrypting sensitive data helps defend against Man-in-The-Middle and other spying attacks when a user (employee) is on a public and/or free Wi-Fi connection. Traditionally, Business Continuity Plans focus on automatic and disaster recovery at the data center level; but that's not all, if employees can no longer access the applications, data, files, and services that are critical to their work, then the business stops, reduce productivity, degrades its image, and lost opportunities until the situation is restored. BYOD policies must include restrictions on the types of applications that may reside on devices that are used to access corporate resources such as email, for example.

Cybersecurity plays an important role in the long-term sustainability of any Organization including those managing the public owned (government) critical infrastructures. In this context, it is increasingly seen as an essential catalyst and the strategy should lie in the quick reaction of the IT department should the attack be perpetrated; how fast would they (IT) implement a solution, taking into account the risks of introducing new solutions knowing that the solution can also fail, and if so, the department should be ready to limit harm to the company, the employees, the users and the State in such an eventuality; BCM cannot be based on a single analysis. But need to think as a process. Performing a long-term analysis, doing trending and setting up a program and making sure the department has the support from the top management. The IT department within which Cyber Security experts work needs to list all risks and processes that may be affected in the event of an incident, makes a list of all the critical processes to restart as soon as possible after an attack. If there is a problem, the department sets priorities and does not try to solve everything at once; how the company intends to address the identified risks, reduce or transfer them (risks) to an insurer for example, or try to prevent to determine the allowable losses itself and, the department should specify the process restart mode and the time to resume. For example, if the services are limited due to a cyberattack, how long will it take to become 100% active again? Traditionally, solutions must remain profitable and the company may not have to move all the staff to another environment or building if teleworking can help them out. But if they go for teleworking, they should consider things like capacity, culture, and security.

However, describing in detail the procedures to be followed in the event of severe attacks already talked about above, that may cause a long interruption of critical processes, and therefore require the activation of the BC plan, Cyber Security experts managing the crisis should ensure that everyone involved is aware of their roles and responsibilities and has been trained to do so. This will greatly accelerate recovery after a disaster. Also Knowing who the stakeholders (if any) are is part of the process, with whom to communicate by making sure there is an up-to-date master plan.

BCM plans should be tested and adapted as necessary. It is not enough to perform one test per year, a permanent monitoring of the BCM process needs to be organised. The ISO 22301 as the main standard of Business Continuity Management places particular emphasis on goal setting, performance measurement and key performance indicators (KPIs) as well, as actions to identify risks and opportunities more quickly. The IT standard in BCM is ISO / IEC 27031.

ISO has been working for some time on an international standard for BCM, ISO 22301, based on existing standards and publications on BCM among others, are the British standards (BS) 25999, ISO Guide 73, ISO 27031 and some other sources. While it is certain that ISO 22301 is not an international version of BS25999-2, the two documents have great similarities. ISO 22301 is one of a series of "Societal Security" (NHS, 2016) standards intended to provide standards for all actors who are affected by an incident impacting the community before, during and after its occurrence. ISO 22301 incorporates the requirements for a BCM system for possible certification. As a result, the Plan-Do-Check-Act (PDCA) cycle is also present in this standard to help the IT and the BCM team to help solve problems more efficiently.

This first standard of a future series is based on the ISO Guide 83, which aims to achieve standardization of management systems standards by standardizing the structure, titles, and texts most frequent. This has allowed critical infrastructures organizations to set more easily a management system integrating various fields; such as quality, Environment, and security and like other ISO standards before, ISO 22301 describes what a critical infrastructure must have to adequately ensure business continuity, taking into account its size, culture and the means available. This standard does not describe how this goal can be achieved; this is the subject of ISO 22313, which is in the process of being written, and which will provide additional information concerning ISO 22301. The ISO 22301 requests to list the requirements of all stakeholders and to take them into account when setting up the BCM system. The organization must, therefore, identify the legislative and regulatory framework to which it subscribes, and its impact must be assessed. The section on crisis communication is also detailed. The ISO 22301 standard section on the assessment of the risks of interruption of critical activities of an organization is perfectly aligned with ISO 31000, the standard for Risk Management. And as a critical infrastructure organization is certified to this standard, they can identify, through gap analysis, complementary steps to fulfil the requirements of ISO 22301.

The new ISO 22301 standard has offered companies management systems, the possibility of integrating the BCM and the ability to respond to incidents that jeopardize the business continuity of the organization which provides added value to the business. As a first step, the company will have a better understanding of how it works, and can better identify its critical processes and products, improve them and make more appropriate strategic choices. Then, in addition to its internal workings, the company will have a clearer view of the expectations of the various stakeholders for it, and can, therefore, react with more agility.

A 5-Step Method

A 5-step method:

- Defines the context, identifies the essential objectives and activities,
- Determines security expectations to meet objectives,
- Identifies, analyses, assesses and treats risks,
- Defines the Business Continuity strategy, and
- Implements and ensures ownership.

The development and implementation of a Business Continuity Plan (BCP) are commonly accepted as risk protection and management actions. In the context of site protection, BCP is pushing for the implementation of real security engineering, which is still too absent in the security process. But looking closely, the BCP carries with it, the seeds of risks that, if denied, can thwart the overall interest of this approach.

The establishment of the BCP is not only for the sole benefit of bringing the company into compliance with legal or regulatory regulations, like in the banking community or public institutions. Whatever the area of the organization in which the Business Continuity Plan is implemented, it brings to it a range of opportunities for the protection of its sites against threats that may affect its activity. The development of a business continuity plan policy requires safety engineering reflection allowing the organization to know vital and critical points. BCP thus prevents the occurrence of malicious acts on its sites and facilities by prioritizing the activities that can be the object of an attack and encourages the evaluation of the measures necessary to remedy them. As a result, it provides a risk analysis methodology complementary to existing security audits. Through this audit exercise that BCP constitutes, the identification of the processes to be secured for business continuity makes it easier for employees to know their organization and makes the dialogue understandable with other public or private establishments (suppliers, customers, etc.). In addition, the different scenarios treated thus make it possible to strengthen site security: for example, PVI (Points of Vital Importance) which can be integrated into the analysis of risks identified by the company's BCP, or security protection of unique production equipment.

Unequivocally, BCP is the lifeline essential to the organization during a major event. However, its very development creates new areas of risk that can aggravate or even provoke a crisis. This can be illustrated in particular by the heterogeneity of crisis management plans: in the event of a building fire, both general safety instructions, evacuation emergency plans and BCP itself can be triggered. All these plans can thus confuse employees on the procedure to follow and in fact, their own security.

BCP identifies essential activities for the proper functioning of any organization by identifying critical resources. To be operational, it must be easily and quickly accessible so that employees can be efficient in the midst of a crisis.

The problem resides within the level of accessibility: for example, obtaining this confidential document with intent to harm a competing business, and terrorists (physical and technological) or its employees, can threaten the survival of the business. It is the same with the internal confidentiality of the company, this vulnerability induced by BCP also concerns dependencies on external providers: for example, the location of backup servers is in itself a vital point of the company. In the case of Cis, sometimes located a few kilometres from the head office, their monitoring and the presence of collaborators on-site not always being optimal, these Datacentre' backups can become a security breach in the protection of critical infrastructures.

RECOVERY PLAN

As with risk analysis methods, continuity and disaster recovery plans following a failure of information systems are common. However, the discovery of a cyberattack plunges organizations or States into a deep crisis despite the existence of these plans and decision-makers often discover cyber risk on this occasion and are not prepared to react. This often leads to bad cascading decisions for example disconnecting all connections or causing a voluntary blackout to completely stop the operation of computers, thus cutting off the internet that further complicates crisis resolution and the clean-up of the attack.

After suffering an attack, a Recovery or Business Continuity Plan must be implemented, depending on the processes the victim has planned in the event of a failure.

Historically, a Business Continuity Plan consists of analysing the impact of the attack or the failure and defining the means to be implemented to limit the damage. Today, it describes all the means intended to ensure the continuity of its business and its applications by guaranteeing high availability. The Disaster Recovery Plan, for its part, describes all the means and procedures to be put in place to ensure rapid recovery of applications after a shutdown, whether it is linked to a technical or electrical fault, an human error, or a disaster.

The vital infrastructure cyber risk analysis particularly illustrates the need for a dialogue at the highest level of government bodies with private operators in charge of those infrastructures, between the security directorates and/or security, the information system security managers and those in charge of risk management. The need for "cross-cooperation" responds to the multiplicity of issues. Cyber threats can have an impact on all aspects of any infrastructure attacked, from its e-reputation to its production capabilities, to the protection of its assets and even the safety of its employees. But more seriously, can have insurmountable consequences on the everyday life of citizens. It is therefore vital to expose the stakes, the nature and specificities of cyber risk to discuss the difficulties of its management from the point of view of critical infrastructures and to open some avenues for reflection to overcome obstacles and develop transversal support; that's what this plan (recovery) is about.

I have done some research and found out that the methods of reviving the activity after a disaster best adapted remain that of "heat" and "cold" which I will try to adapt to the current context by giving more details of how they work and propose some revisions for vital infrastructures after an attack for a quick recovery response.

- Heat: from a synchronous or asynchronous copy of the infrastructure data, relying on the last coherent state. The start-up of the standby servers is accelerated by replicating the data and trying to obtain a state as close as possible to that of the last moment before the failure. Thus, the time required to restart applications can be limited to a few minutes.

- Cold: the restart is made from the latest backups of the company. The company then restores its data ex-nihilo from their backup media and restarts its applications. This solution is more economical than a hot recovery plan. The time to restart is slower: several hours or even days. With disk-based backups, this delay can be reduced to 2 hours. This delay also depends on the frequency of backups.

For this, redundant equipment must be implemented in several data centers so that in case of failure of the infrastructure of the company, the relay can be taken automatically by the backup site. But to stay within the framework of vital infrastructures, for all these methods to be effective, it is however in the interest of the companies in charge of these infrastructures to organize a crisis management exercise with all the internal actors concerned. for example, with management and legal services, as well as with third parties, such as specialized lawyers and experts in post-incident technical analysis, established by each State of the European Union, including the United Kingdom, which may include being grouped in a "Central Office for Combating Information" and "Communication Technologies Crime", which will coordinate their actions with, for example, an "Information technology fraud investigation team", or with an "Information systems security agency" with headquarters in each State, to benefit from cooperation with an "intelligence-led internal intelligence centre" and the network for example.

EVALUATION
APPROACH TO
DEVELOP RESILIENCE

Developments in recent years, particularly the situation in Crimea, the line of tension between Ukraine and Russia and the rise of ISIL or DAECH, reflect a shift in the strategic environment, which encourages Europe through its NATO alliance to strengthen its posture of deterrence and defense. At the same time, the civilian population and critical infrastructure, largely owned by the private sector, continue to be the target of terrorist or hybrid threats including cyberattacks. This commitment is based on the recognition that the strategic environment has evolved, and that the resilience of structures, resources and civil services is the first line of defense for modern societies today, and all countries that have put in place a real resilience policy, and where all levels of the state, as well as the public and private sectors, are involved in civil sector preparedness planning, have fewer vulnerabilities be used as a means of pressure or to be targeted by opponents.

Resilience is therefore an important aspect of deterrence by prohibition; that is, persuading an opponent not to attack by convincing him that an attack will not allow him to achieve his goals. This resilience policy has the advantage of rebounding after crises. It allows eventual victims to generally recover more quickly and can return to their pre-crisis level of functioning with greater ease than other less resilient ones. As a result, the continuity of public authorities and services essential to the population is ensured more sustainably, and the ability of the civilian sector to support a NATO military operation as well as the ability to rapidly provide reinforcements to an ally is reinforced. This level of resilience is useful in the face of the full range of threats, whether to counter a terrorist attack or respond to it, or for possible scenarios of collective defense. Improving resilience through civilian sector preparedness, therefore, plays an important role in strengthening the Alliance's deterrence and defense posture. Given the importance it places on resilience, Europe is now focusing on early warning capabilities in the work on its civilian sector preparedness within the NATO alliance and partners, which implies improving situational awareness and readiness for possible incidents or possible attacks. Europe (including the UK) nevertheless maintains its ability to respond to serious civil emergencies. For example, in the event of an earthquake, devastating forest fire or severe flood, or in the event of a human-caused disaster, the main NATO response mechanism to civilian emergencies, the Euro-Atlantic Centre Disaster Response Coordination, may, on request, co-ordinate assistance to the Allied or Disaster Partner. Societies are extremely complex, their vital sectors and services are interdependent and inseparable. They rely on support infrastructures that are essential to their operation but assume that these infrastructures can withstand disturbances. The supply of goods and services is determined almost exclusively by supply and demand and is generally based on the "just in time" model. Internet communication systems and logistics are also fundamental for the production, trade and supply of goods and services.

A high level of interconnection can increase efficiency and achieve economies of scale, but the greater the interdependencies, the higher the risk of a domino effect in case of disturbance.

While national authorities may rely on a legislative and regulatory framework, they have little power to act directly on private/commercial procurement, except in emergencies. Since the system seems to work well, national authorities have little reason to be directly involved. The responsibility to solve any supply problem is therefore mainly left to the industry. Public authorities are primarily concerned with ensuring the levels of safety and quality of goods and services, especially food and other consumer goods. The European Union plays a very important role in the way public administration is structured for these sectors. Its directives and regulations have largely shaped the plans of its Member States and the commercial sector. Emergency planning, which aims to ensure the smooth running and continuation of operations, focuses on the ability to deal with the most likely short-term disruptions. The commercial sector has focused on minimizing its costs in the face of such disruptions, rather than preparing for larger emergencies that have a domino effect across sectors and proper sectors' society. The European project H2020 IMPROVER (Improved risk evaluation and implementation of resilience concepts to critical infrastructure) aims to improve the resilience of so-called "critical" infrastructures. Critical infrastructures (or CIs) include any equipment, system or part of a system whose functioning is essential for the maintenance of vital societal functions (Theocharidou et al., 2016; Moteff, 2012). Transport networks (air, road, etc.), electricity and water or gas distribution networks, medical services, computer servers, etc. are considered to be CIs. When they are prone to crises, the vital functions provided by CIs must be restored or adapted as quickly as possible to return to a minimum level of functioning required. This ability to maintain or restore minimum functioning despite disturbances refers to the concept of resilience. It is then necessary for managers of CIs to determine the resilience of these CIs in the face of various critical events to identify possible improvement actions. The notion of resilience tends to take an increasingly important place in the management of CIs as well as security. Knowing the resilience' capacity of CIs, therefore, requires looking not only at the safety of users and residents but also at the societal and economic consequences that can result from a lasting interruption of services.

This book presents the formal methodology developed within the framework of the IMPROVER project for the evaluation of the resilience of CIs, It analyzes it and proposes solutions. The analysis made it possible to demonstrate that resilience is apprehended by a wide variety of indicators, often poorly formalized, on which no consensus has been reached. Some methodologies for assessing resilience can be found in the publication by Hosseini et al. (2016), where a non-exhaustive state of the art of qualitative (like that proposed by Kahan et al. (2009)) and quantitative (like that of Bruneau et al. (2003)) evaluation methods are presented. One of the research axes of the IMPROVER project focused on the development of a methodology for evaluating societal, organizational and technological resilience for all types of CI; and this, whatever the hazard to which CIs are exposed. This evaluation must make it possible to measure the capacity of a CI to resist or to have a minimum residual resistance during an exceptional natural or anthropic critical event. In the framework of the IMPROVER project, Pursiainen et al. (2016) proposed a holistic methodology called CIRI (Critical Infrastructure Resilience Index) to assess overall resilience. This method aims to estimate the resilience of CIs by taking into account the context defined by the following parameters:

- The area of resilience studied (organizational, societal or technological);
- The type of hazard considered (natural, anthropogenic, malicious act, etc.);
- Situational factors (peak consumption, time of year, season, etc.).

This methodology is based on the conceptualization of CI resilience in the form of a hierarchical structure with at the top (level 0) the CIRI which is then subdivided at level 1 into

7 indicators representing the resilience associated with each phase/aspect of the risk management; namely: risk assessment, prevention, crisis preparedness, monitoring and alert systems, crisis response, infrastructure recovery and post-crisis learning (UNISDR, 2009). These 7 level 1 indicators are in turn broken down into at least 2 sub-levels (2 and 3), to describe their generic areas of application as finely as possible and thus make them easier to measure. If necessary, the level of decomposition can be increased to be able to apply the generic indicators to a sector or a structure (for example, a specific bridge of a highway) and/ or to a scenario (for example, an accident on a pile deck). It is up to managers to choose to aggregate the indicators before a global analysis or else to focus on the indicators at each level of the hierarchical structure; the latter approach can be more informative to identify gaps in resilience. Table 5 shows an example of the meaning that could be given to the performance values obtained for the level 2

Indicator "Trigger thresholds".
Indicator level 2
Indicator level 1
CIRI =   0

Performance Values Obtained for the level 2 indicator "Trigger thresholds".

Table 5: Scoring grid for level 2 criterion "Trigger thresholds" (Pursiainen et al, 2016)

Note	Meaning	Description
0	Non existant	Thresholds do not prevent danger
1	Initial / Ad hoc	The thresholds are exceeded

		during the occurrence of a danger
2	Reproducible but intuitive	The thresholds allow to anticipate a danger but the crisis management is carried out in emergency
3	Defined process	The thresholds allow crisis management according to a defined procedure
4	Managed and measurable	Thresholds limit the impact of a hazard on the IC service
5	Optimized	Thresholds are used to organize remediation so that no impact on the functioning of the CI is observed

A representation in the form of a cobweb provides a visual illustration instantly giving strengths and areas for improvement in CI. In the example presented in Table 5, representing the level 1 indicators, the CI presents significant opportunities for improvement in terms of its surveillance and alarm systems and terms of the means implemented for post-crisis learning; however, the risk analysis is a strong point.

The objective of this example is to illustrate the methodology developed by applying it to the evaluation of the level 1 indicator "Surveillance and alarm systems". An integral part of risk management procedures, surveillance and alarm systems are recommended in the concepts of technological resilience for their contribution in all crisis phases (NF ISO 31 000): continuous monitoring, pre-events, detection of a crisis and feedback based on the data recorded.

The breakdown of the main indicators is delicate because it must aim, except for its lowest level, at the comprehensiveness of the application of the concepts. The flexibility granted by the lowest level allows the method to be adapted to all situations and all types of CI. The methodology proposed by Pursiainen et al. (2016) is characterized by certain flexibility of generic decompositions in very different contexts. This project focuses on the level 1 indicator "Monitoring and alarm systems", which has enabled a breakdown into generic level 2 and 3 indicators (Figure 1). However, it should be clarified that all the generic indicators of levels 2 and 3 may not necessarily apply to all the cases studied.

Breakdown of the Resilience Indicator

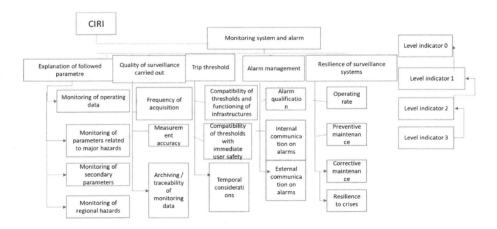

Figure 1: Breakdown of the resilience indicator "Monitoring and alarm systems" (Pursiainen et al., 2016)

ETHICAL
CONSIDERATIONS

Preparing for a cyber-attack assumes a balance between the interests of individuals and the interests of society, which may be divergent. In emergencies, the individual enjoyment of human rights and civil liberties may need to be limited by the public interest. However, the desire to protect individual rights must be an integral part of any policy. Measures that limit individual rights and civil liberties must be necessary, reasonable, proportionate, equitable, non-discriminatory and fully by national laws and international treaties. Ethical principles are tools to evaluate applications contradictory and to reach appropriate decisions. Ethics does not provide a set of frozen policies; ethical considerations will be rather shaped by local context and values cultural. The principles of equity, utility, efficiency, freedom, reciprocity and solidarity are particularly useful in the context of preparing for a cyber-attack. Although they often result in contradictory requirements, they provide a framework for stakeholders/actors to assess and balance the range of interests that flow from them. All ethical deliberations must take place in the context of principles governing human rights, and all policies must be consistent with applicable human rights law.

LITERATURE
REVIEW

The methodology proposed in this book for the identification and localization of critical infrastructures and their protection is based on a set of criteria derived from the analysis of "territorial criticality". It implements through a study, a developed analysis grid. A political criticality analysis will be developed based on the example of the consultation process between the European Commission and its member of States, plus the UK, aimed at defining the criteria for identifying critical infrastructure: the criticality criteria used on the gravity of potential consequences following the malfunction or the shutdown of infrastructure after a cyber-attack. This work highlights the key elements of the consultation process, in particular the definition of criticality thresholds for consequences. It proposes an application of the criteria retained for the identification of CIs. The cases studied and highlighted in this book relate to critical infrastructures and the attacks carried out against them; for example the malfunction of a pumping station located on a set of trans-European gas pipelines after an attack, the malfunction of a signal lights of railway systems or a power plant hijacked by means of a simple Ransomware or DoS Attack etc.

Europe and the UK became interested later than the United States in implementing policies to protect critical infrastructure. Indeed, the EU was first oriented towards the establishment of an area of economic cooperation. In addition, the UE did not have the authority to intervene in the security field. However, socio-economic developments, as well as the consideration of the terrorist threat have favoured the initiation of reflection on the protection of CIs by the EU and the UK. The EU first took an interest in infrastructure and its role in the structure of the single market. The aim was to promote trade between the Member States and to develop a large internal market. EU policy has therefore mainly focused on opening up the services market to competition and the liberalization of the infrastructure sector, in particular for the energy, communications and transport sectors (Bouchon, 2005). However, the increasing interconnection of European infrastructures has made European authorities aware of the possible cross-border damage in the event of a crisis linked to a sudden and disastrous attack. The EU then took an interest in the protection and security of citizens. It first sought to harmonize the multiple national regulatory systems guaranteeing the security of trade and products. Faced with the difficulty of the task, a new approach was put in place in 1985: the committee decided to stick, domain by domain, to the promulgation of a certain number of essential requirements, mainly relating to security products put into circulation. It thus referred to the States themselves, the task of attesting the conformity of the products to the notified requirements (Galland, 2007). But, due to the growing threat, it soon became apparent that these measures were insufficient for the protection of the infrastructure itself.

In June 2004, three months after the Madrid attacks which left 191 dead, the European Council asked its commission to consider an overall strategy for the protection of European CIs. In response, the commission issued a communication entitled "Protecting Critical Infrastructure in the Fight Against Terrorism" (COM 2004). To prepare a European program for the protection of critical infrastructure (EPPCI). In November 2005, the commission published a "green book" for a CI protection program (COM 2005). The objective of this book was to propose questions, present ideas and collect contributions from the main actors, to define the EPPCI. In December 2006, the committee adopted the "Communication on a European program for the protection of critical infrastructures" (COM, 2006), which sets out the principles and the procedures of an EPPCI. In December 2006, the committee adopted the "Communication on a European program for the protection of critical infrastructures" (COM, 2006), which sets out the principles and the procedures of an EPPCI. And the Directive on "identification and classification of European critical infrastructure as well as the assessment of the need to improve their protection" (Directive 2008) is the main device and was adopted by the 2008 European Council. In addition to the Directive, the EPPCI proposes an action plan, for an alert network concerning critical infrastructures, the establishment of expert groups at the EU level, procedures for sharing information concerning the protection of CIs, it also proposes to consider accompanying financial measures within the framework of the specific program "Prevention, security-related risks".

The reflection on the current modalities of the protection of critical infrastructures marks a real break with the previous conceptions of security, as evidenced by the doctrine of "global security" implemented by the Council of the EU. This is defined as the "ability to provide a given community and its members with a level of protection against risks and threats of all kinds" (Ocqueteau, 2007). Four aspects make it possible to characterize the rupture.

1. The doctrine of "global security" first refers to the questioning of the relationship between security policy and military activities (Winkler, 2004). It is no longer a question of fighting against clearly identified external enemies but against vulnerabilities inherent in civil society, which are no longer expressed in terms

of conflicts but in terms of risks.

2. This questioning also upsets the idea that security is only linked to extraordinary circumstances such as wars for example. The protection of its CIs refers to a vision of daily security, which is not the security of the nation but that of the citizens and the economic world (Foot, 2004). It attests to the transition from a reactive security system, in response to an assault, to a preventive security system (Houska, 2004).

3. The rupture questions the distinction between public and private in the management of security. Traditionally, it is up to the State to ensure security, which is positioned at the heart of its regalian functions (Aubouin, 1997). However, with the protection of critical infrastructures, Kristensen shows that from now on, security also concerns the domestic space and requires the commitment of public and private actors who become fundamental actors of security (Dunn Cavelly, Kristensen, 2008).

4. Finally, Bigo's work on the geographical extension of internal security within the national space shows the need to consider the links between security and the territory. He insists on the fact that the security of the territory is no longer limited only to its borders but also concerns spaces located inside the national space, and critical infrastructures (Bigo 1994, 2000). With the development of cybercrime, the space to be protected also becomes virtual (Houska, 2004). It is, therefore, necessary to think of the emergence of the protection of critical infrastructures in politics as a phenomenon of "continuity in discontinuity" (Aradau, Van Munster, 2007).

METHODOLOGY

Research stages and process

The first step in the research was to define the conceptual models on which to base a methodological approach to identifying critical infrastructures (CIs): a criticality model and criticality spaces, a vulnerability model, a multi-scalar analysis model of infrastructure.

From these models, was born an interrogation on the criteria of territorial criticality being able to allow the evaluation of the criticality of an infrastructure. Identification of three criteria: criteria related to the importance of service, criteria of the criticality of physical or technological terrorism, and criteria related to the gravity of the consequences. Then, these criteria were integrated into the framework of a methodology allowing to guide the process of identification of CIs. It was, therefore, necessary to adopt the point of view of professionals responsible for the protection of critical infrastructures, facing their area of competence and all of its infrastructures. From there, it was possible to build an approach as a set of spatial filters, allowing step by step, to lead to the identification of CIs within the UK territory while taking into account the point of view of actors across the weight given to the indicators in the context of multi-criteria analysis. To test the validity of this methodology, it was applied to the cases of energy CIs located in the territory of the European Union and the UK.

FINDINGS

Research has also led to the findings that new information and communication technologies have become predominant in the lives of States, and citizens. This communication space called cyberspace is constituted by the global interconnection of computerized data processing equipment of digital data. It is thus a mesh network of infrastructures (Information Technologies, Telecommunications Networks, Computer Systems) that can become vulnerable when it is the object of attacks whose damage is difficult to assess, especially when they touch whole areas of activity. The State's vital industries and infrastructure rely on these information systems, subject to multiple cybernetic attacks, sometimes serious, altering or weakening these systems.

However, It is impossible indeed to secure what is not visible by relying on traditional approaches that consist of managing network security, relying primarily on manual processes, and pre-established strategies to identify and block attacks. Therefore, Other techniques like Artificial Intelligence and machine learning, Big Data and Cloud computing will also be considered: Surveys conducted among the IT professionals and decision-makers are highly determinative to achieve the objectives of this research. the collected data are an added value that helps to determine the most appropriate tools to deal with and repel cyberattacks but also to implement a resilience policy to mitigate the impact of a possible attack. The purpose of this survey is to take stock of the resistance policies put in place by these firms, whom the teams sometimes have the heavy task of protecting the country against cybernetic attacks and, to be able from returning data to suggest solutions. The method is simple short and not expensive. It assesses the risks to potential victims in real-time. It consists of collecting and interpreting quantitative and qualitative data.

For logistical reasons, the survey was conducted only in the UK

➢ The population surveyed: decision-makers of companies in charge of the IT strategy.

➢ The survey was conducted from May 8, 2019, to February 21, 2020.

➢ 502 decision-makers from 106 companies and industries in the UK, answered all the questions, as corporate officers (general managers), or as directors or financial officers but also as IT managers, including 6 industries considered to be among the largest and most important critical industries in the UK classified as on "high risk" if attacked, 60 industries which I will classify as on "medium risk" if attacked, and 40 industries are as on "low risk" critical infrastructures

However, the classification as "low risk" above does NOT in any way mean that a cyberattack against this category of industries will have a low effect. Regardless of the classification level, a cyberattack on one of them will considerably cripple the UK economy, impact with immeasurable consequences the everyday life of its citizens and alter the reputation of the company and that of the State and this is also true for all European countries

➢ At the end of the survey, the aggregated results were analyzed to be able to easily detect flaws and make recommendations..

RESULTS

Sample Structure: Profile of respondents:

➤ *Table 6: Profile of respondents (From Own Survey, Data collected from 8 May 2019-21 Feb 2020-UK)*

IT managers	48%
financial officers	22%
general managers	30%

➤ SIZE OF COMPANIES:

➤ *Table 7: Size of companies (From Own Survey, Data collected from May 8, 19-Feb 21, 2020-UK)*

Very small businesses (Micro-Business): less than $5 million of turnover 0-9 employees	**43%**
SMEs (small and medium-sized enterprises): No more than $10 million turnover less or equal 50 employees	**26%**
Mid-sized Businesses (MSBs): from $100 million of turnover about 250 employees	**21%**
Large companies: more than 3 billion dollars of turnover, from 250 employees	**10%**

Figure representative of the results on the above table 7

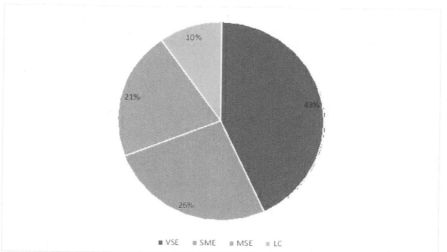

Figure 2: Size of companies (From Own Survey, Data collected from 8 May 19-21 Feb 20-UK)

SURVEY RESULTS

From the question: Q: Has your company ever experienced an attempt to cyberattack?

- ✓ Answer: 43% of respondents have already had one or more attempts or attack against their network.

Total Of respondents

- ✓ 43% of respondents have already had one or more attempts or attack against their network.
- ☐ 57% of respondents have never been attacked OR ignored it. Fig 3.

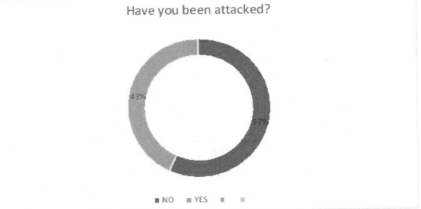

Figure 3: Respondents been attacked (From Own Survey, Data collected from 8May 19-21 Feb 20-UK).

For question

Q: What negative effects has your company experienced as a result of cyberattacks?

- ✓ Answer. 97% of companies that have already experienced cyberattacks suffered from these attacks fig 4.

Respondents who have experienced cyberattack

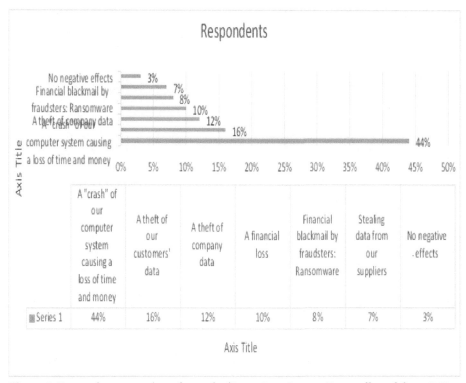

Figure 4: Respondents experienced attacks (From Own Survey, Data collected from 8 May 19-21 Feb 20-UK)

Unfortunately, it is exceptional for a company that has been hacked to come out without any damage.

According to this survey, 97% of companies been hacked, suffers one or more prejudices: total shutdown of their system, data theft (from the company / its customers/suppliers), blackmail ... Regarding this last point, it is impressive that 8% of pirated companies have already been victims of a "ransomware" (software that

Take control over the company's system that he has infected and that requires a ransom of a ransom to release it).

Q: At what level do you estimate the risk that your company being "cyber" attacked over the years to come?

> With the exception of large groups, all companies underestimate the risks of cyber-attack. Fig 5.

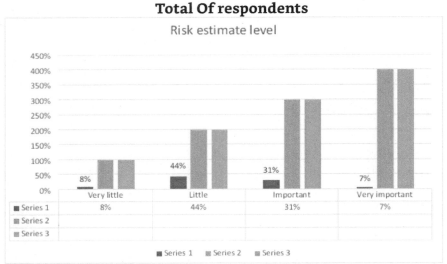

Figure 5: Estimate level of risk (From Own Survey, Data collected from 8 May 19-21 Feb 20-UK)

Breakdown of results by type of company:

Table 8: Breakdown of results by type of company (From Own Survey, Data collected from May 19-Feb 20-UK)

	Risk very insignific ant	Risk low	Risk Import ant	Risk very import ant
Very small businesses: less than $5 million dollars of turnover	24%	60%	15%	1%
SMEs (small	13%	45%	33%	9%

and medium-sized enterprises): from 5 to 10 million dollars turnover				
MSE (medium-sized enterprises): from 100 million to 3 billion dollars of turnover	7%	34%	48%	11%
Large companies: more than 3 billion dollars of turnover	0%	13%	87%	0%

Given these results, there is the impression that society is really at the heart of a structured organization that leads the targeted attacks even if the motivations are still not the same for each of these attacks. Some victims are not even aware that they have been cyber-attacked. Many of those who do not know have answered "I do not know" or "I'm not sure" which shows the level of lack of training but worse lack of policy that should govern and structure their company.

The decision-makers of big companies appear to be conscious of an imminent attack. However, 38% of the decision-makers consider the risk of the attack "important" or "very important" even though 43% of companies have already been victims of cyberattacks. On the other hand, it should be noted that SME managers strongly underestimate the risks associated with cyber security. And when the question of whether they felt their businesses were better protected today, the mixed answers left me perplexed but not surprised; Small businesses answered "no" for about 50% while large firms' decision-makers all answered "yes".

For the question

Q: Do you think that today your company is well protected against cyberattack?

All respondents fig 6.

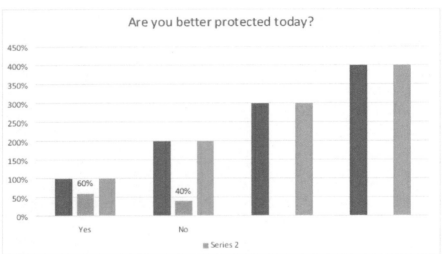

Figure 6: Those that are better protected (From Own Survey, Data collected from May-19 to Feb 20-UK)

But these results are not thinkable as 40% of respondents answered "NO" which means, they are aware of the danger to be exposed to a cyberattack. They acknowledge the existence of a real risk, but what are they waiting to protect themselves? many of these respondents still think that their anti-virus software would be enough to protect them against a cyberattack. So for them, it all depends on how effective their anti-virus is. This explains the answer part of this 40% of respondents answering "I don't know".

Breakdown of results by company:

Table 9: Breakdown of results by company (From Own Survey, Data collected from 8 May 19-21 Feb 20-UK)

	YES	NO
Very small businesses (Micro-Business): less than £1 million of turnover 0-9 employees	47%	43%
SMEs (small and medium-sized enterprises): No more than £6.5 million turnover less or equal 50 employees	74%	26%
Mid-sized Businesses (MSBs): from 50 million to £25-500 million of turnover about 250 employees	79%	21%
Large companies: more than 1.5 billion pounds of turnover, from 250 employees	99%	1%

To the question of whether these professionals have put in place meaningful measures to deal with cyberattacks, it was noted that the protection by anti-virus and firewall protection enabled were the most used. The network access codes, which is the authentication procedure, only come in the third rank. However, these access codes are not regularly changed either.

For the question: Q: What cybersecurity measures have you adopted to deal with cyberattacks? Fig 7.

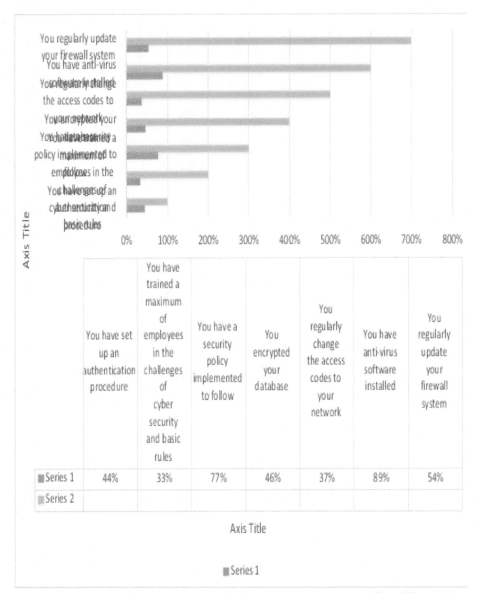

Figure 7: Measures to deal with cyberattacks (From Own Survey, Data collected from 8 May 19-21 Feb 20-UK).

One of the most important questions for me as the investigator was whether these managers order at least a periodic assessment of resilience through internal analyses and audits and/or external including intrusion tests but also detection devices incidents to make sure their systems are working properly. But the different answers obtained are alarming and the question was simply short and precise so that they understand the meaning of it.

For question: Q. Do you usually carry out intrusion tests? If yes how many per year?
All respondents: fig 8.

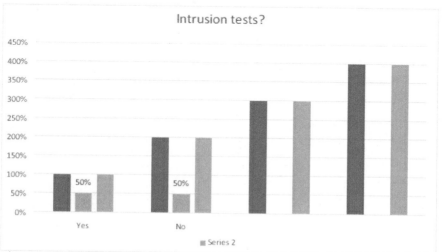

Figure 8: Do your company usually do intrusion tests (From Own Survey, Data collected from 8 May 19-21 Feb 20-UK)

Table 11: Number of intrusion tests ordered (Own Survey, Data collected from 8 May 19-21 Feb 20-UK)

How much tests have you ordered within	6 months	1 year
Very small businesses (Micro-Business): less than £1 million of turnover 0-9 employees	0	0
SMEs (small and medium-sized enterprises): No more than £6.5 million turnover less or equal 50 employees	0	0

Mid-sized Businesses (MSBs): from 50 million to £25-500 million of turnover about 250 employees	0 – 1	1
Large companies: more than 1.5 billion pounds of turnover, from 250 employees	1	2 – 3

The last question asked was about business continuity. This is a key issue and of great importance, essential to the survival of an organization

For the question: Q. What would you do if your security has been compromised? Do you have a Business continuity plan (BCP) in place? Table 12.

Table 12: Business continuity plan implemented (from Own survey, Data collected from 8-21 May 2019-UK)

Do you have a BCP?	Yes	No	Not Sure
Respondents	50%	22%	28%

The results obtained from the table 6 above are translate into the graph below on figure 9.

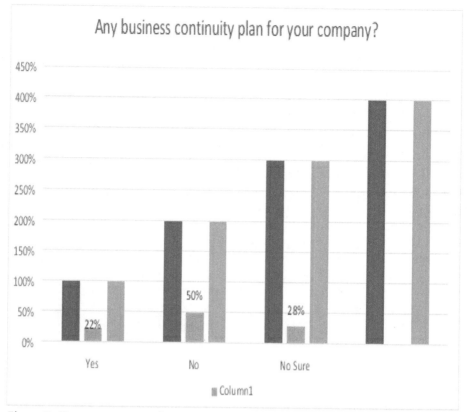

Figure 9: Has your company have a Business continuity plan (from Own survey, Data collected from May 19-21 Feb 20-UK)

The essence of the survey method can be explained as "questioning individuals on a topic or topics and then describing their responses" Jackson, S.L. (2011). The main purpose of this method is to describe certain aspects or characteristics of the population and/or test hypotheses about the nature of relationships within a population. The method used to collect the data is simple and is based on physical contact with the respondents. A questionnaire is provided to them to answer any of the questions of their choice, without any pressure and in freedom.

This questionnaire is submitted particularly to the heads of companies, the managers, and the IT managers but also to the managers in charge of risk management teams; within small,

small and medium-sized enterprises and in large companies (most of them are critical infrastructure companies). The collected samples are then analyzed and interpreted in the form of graphs and tables to evaluate the rationality of the results obtained. The purpose of this method is realized to collect a large amount of information in a short time, and Sample group members can remain anonymous. This method is simple and cheap compared to some other methods because it allows the possibility to generate a large amount of data, but also presents some difficulties to deepen the research, and the selection of the first choice Denscombe (2010).

CHAPTER 4

- ❖ **Data Analysis**
- ❖ **Discussion**
- ❖ **Conclusions**
- ❖ **Recommendations**
- ❖ **Glossary**
- ❖ **References**
- ❖ **Biography**
- ❖ **Appendix A Plan**

DATA ANALYSIS

The goal should be to make the company resilient to the risk of loss or compromise of information. Companies are subject to many laws and regulations, many of which require the implementation of appropriate security controls. in this scenario, it is shown that the human is at the center of the security of his company and that a single error posed by him can be disastrous. The method used to collect the data shows that the results obtained undoubtedly highlighted some security issues given the context in which cybernetic attacks are observed against vital infrastructure.

This survey is a sample of the state of mind that lives within some IT professionals or decision-makers and even unfortunately managing directors of all these firms that often are also those who are in charge of vital infrastructures on which our new society relies. in this survey, the results obtained speak for themselves, and the worst is that even those companies that have a security policy in place do not read them. it is often emphasized the training of employees within these policies but no one pays attention.

Simple rules that could prove useful to counter an attack DDoS or WannaCry ransomware attacks are simply neglected. Asked if they have a safety policy in place, more than two-thirds of respondents said that their institution has a security policy in place, a number that is not far from those who say they have been subjected to a cyberattack: a real paradox.

The method of evaluation used has upstream consisted of two issues: the first was to ensure that I obtain the expected result, that is to say, the information I needed downstream to be able to analyze it, the second thing was to know if I had the resources required to carry out this investigation.

In theory, it was necessary to determine what I wanted to know before choosing the

methodology. Too often, and for that, I had taken into account the accessibility as to the method to choose by limiting the scope of the research realistically. So I considered both what I wanted to know and what I could achieve with my resources, to determine the orientation and methods of this book. The resources available to me included access to specific groups of people, most of whom were IT professionals, with different backgrounds like the network security team, risk management team and decision-makers.

This was a qualitative survey method. I chose individual interviews and structured face-to-face interviews. They were carried out on company premises and operated on a structured continuum. This survey gave me direct information from people who know

the most about it. These are not results obtained by computer simulation but real facts and reliable results. It is the key point of the interviews: these interviews have been pre-booked and scheduled after getting all key participants on the phone.

Before conducting the interview, I needed first to establish an "interview schedule" of questions and obtain an agreement with the interviewee which could be extended further accordingly depending on the answers of the interviewee. These talks provided me with more in-depth data allowing a relationship to develop where thoughts, ideas, feelings, emotions, attitudes and responses were captured and put into context.

Before beginning, it was important to adhere to the appropriate ethical guidelines and obtain 'informed consent' from the interviewee via a signed form stating that the interviewee understands the purpose of the interview. Foremost, the data would be used for research material, thereafter, the informed consent document would be kept open till the end of the research. The information was filtered through their perceptions of reality as some of them only started to realize the impact that an attack could cause on the safety of the employees.

During these interviews, a digital recording was used to reassure respondents that anything they say will be retained and anything they don't will not be reported. This is what I called the "data reliability method". The questionnaire was planned and designed carefully to collect the information for data analysis thereafter. It consisted of a list of questions, which was open. During the design, the costs were also considered, its production, its purpose, organization, schedule, length, permission, ethics, construction, wording and the audience (Denscombe, 2007).

Data collected and analyzed in this book are based on what I was told by professionals from companies that I visited, but the perceptions of the interviewees were also considered. I had the opportunity to visit some data centers, and their computer rooms; I could see data connection points from the walls. I'd like to dwell on this specific point a bit: data points and wall plates are common in homes to help bridge data connections; they can be used for Wi-Fi networking to media devices, where data points extend and connect. The wall plates cover the electrical wires and cables from the datapoint outlet. Data points are a network cable (CAT6) going from one place to another. They can be very dangerous when open, when the service listening on the port is misconfigured, unpatched, vulnerable to exploits or have poor network security rules. Additionally, open ports provide a larger "attack surface" or opportunity for an attacker to find vulnerabilities, exploits, misconfigurations, and other risks due to network communication allowed on a specific network port.

My work had also consisted of pre-determining the categories of behavior that interested me the most, to better structure my approach. I was more interested in the method of "qualitative research" rather than "quantitative research", to observe natural settings and understand the culture and processes of the Interviewees. An observation schedule was dressed and the interviewees were informed: conducting systematic observations required consent from the participant involved. However, when people know that they are being observed, they behave differently. So I took this into account as well when analyzing the data. The results obtained while classifying data using an initial data set, support the findings. It can therefore be said that data classification can be used to detect abnormal behavior in critical infrastructures and achieve a high success rate when identifying normal behaviors.

DISCUSSION

The convergence of industrial technologies OT (Operational Technology) and information technologies (IT) weighs on the security of industrial control systems and SCADA. With this decompartmentalization, these systems are exposed to a universe of rapidly expanding threats and constitute targets for hackers potentially involved in terrorism, cyberwar or espionage. Attacks on risky infrastructure (power plants, factories, sewage treatment plants, oil platforms or road traffic control systems) can pose a serious threat to national security, but can also lead to serious financial losses, the risk of " A tarnished reputation for businesses victims of the attack, or even of human losses.

The permanent behavior analysis provides monitoring information to the security teams. A centralized security tool provides logging, reporting and analytical processing operations while evaluating the activity information collected on the entire system. The tool also offers management of security information and events, as well as automation of security orchestration tasks and remediation functions. Behavioral analysis of users and devices and threat assessment provides ongoing protection.

SCADA refers to a category of software dedicated to controlling industrial processes and collecting data in real-time in remote locations. SCADA systems can be used to maintain control over the equipment, and industrial processes, and to optimize their operating conditions. A typical SCADA system is composed of transmitters, a remote terminal unit (RTU), communication protocols allowing communication between servers and RTU transmitters, a data server intended for data archiving. and to supply the human-machine interfaces (HMI). HMIs are user interfaces that can link the operator to the control device of an industrial system. If a SCADA automation infrastructure is properly designed, it should enable companies to better respond to operational questions, do more, do it better and cheaply, increase the availability and life cycle of their equipment, improve performance and reduce maintenance costs for their equipment.

Previously, manufacturers have used minicomputers to optimize their processes and equipment. At the time, monolithic SCADA systems were very popular and did not use common network services. The systems were therefore independent, that is, a computer could not connect to other systems. Remote sites were connected via a backup mainframe system. This ensured the redundancy of the first generation SCADA system. The monolithic concept was mainly used in case of failure of the primary mainframe system. The use of this old form of SCADA system was limited to monitoring the system sensors as well as signalling any operation if the programmed alarm levels were exceeded. Then came the second generation of SCADA systems, the sharing of control functions was distributed among several systems connected to each other via a local area network (LAN). They were therefore called distributed SCADA systems. Individual stations were used to share information in real-time, process orders, and perform control tasks to trigger alarm levels in the event of problems. What sets them apart from older systems is the reduced cost and size of the station. However, network protocols were not standardized and installation security could only be determined by very few people outside of the developers. In other words, the security of the second generation SCADA installation has been ignored. As already said, today's SCADA systems are now networked and can communicate over a wide area network (WAN) over data lines or the phone. These systems typically use Ethernet or fibre-optic connections to transmit data between nodes. They also use programmable logic controllers (PLCs) to monitor or adjust routine signalling systems in the event of important decisions. If the first and second generation SCADA systems were limited to single networks or buildings, the third generation SCADA uses the Internet, which often involves a security problem.

However, the advent of the fourth generation of SCADA systems has drastically reduced the cost of infrastructure through the adoption of internet of things (IoT) technology and cloud computing. The integration and maintenance of systems are therefore very easy, compared to that of previous systems. The latest technological advancements in SCADA systems are now making it possible to produce real-time status reports, use more complex control algorithms and strengthen the security of sensitive information in large companies. In addition, these systems can be implemented on traditional PLCs. As mentioned, SCADA is a term used to refer to centralized systems designed to control and monitor an entire industrial site or complex equipment spread over large areas. Almost all control actions are performed automatically by PLCs or Remote Terminal Units (RTUs). Take the example of an industrial water supply process: the PLC can in this case-control the cooling water flow and the SCADA system can record and display all changes related to alarm conditions in case of variations or loss of flow, significant rise in temperature, etc. Data are collected at the level of an application programming interface or an RTU. They include the status reports of the monitored equipment as well as the meter readings. They will then be formatted so that the operator of the control room can take the necessary measures to add or override normal PLC commands (RTU), using a Human Machine Interface (HMI). Thus, the RTU can connect to the physical equipment and convert all the electrical signals coming from this equipment into digital values, such as the open or closed state of a valve or switch, flow or pressure, current-voltage, etc. In this way, the RTU can automatically control the equipment or allow an operator to do so, for example by closing or opening a valve or switch, or by adjusting the speed of the pump. Mention should be made of what the HMI means. It is a device that provides data processed by the RTU to the human operator. The latter can therefore use it to control industrial processes. The HMI is linked to the SCADA system databases, which allows it to display diagnostic data, management information, logistics information, detailed diagrams of the operation of a given machine or sensor, maintenance procedures or troubleshooting guides. The operator can therefore have, for example, the image of a pump connected to the piping. The HMI provides him with a diagram showing whether this pump works or not, or whether the quantity of liquid pumped through the piping complies with the operating conditions of the equipment at a given time. In the event of an adjustment, for example, when a pump is stopped, the HMI software will instantly show the reduction in the flow of fluid in the pipes.

The block diagrams provided by the HMI may be in the form of digital photographs of the process equipment and be accompanied by animated symbols (schematic symbols, line graphics, etc.). As a result, representations can be as simple as an on-screen traffic light network, representing the state of the traffic light in real-time in a given area. They can also be very complex, such as the multi-projector display representing the position of all trains on a vast network of railways.

Generally speaking, SCADA systems are used in alarm systems, which means that there are only two digital status points. On the one hand, when the alarm requirements are satisfied, it activates. If necessary, it remains in its state. In other words, they look like the car's fuel level alarm system. When the tank is almost empty, the alarm activates automatically in the form of a light signal. As for SCADA systems, the operators and managers of the company are notified by text messages and e-mails sent with the activation of the alarm. But in addition, they can view graphic trends, and manage the various parameters relating to the configuration of their equipment. In these different sectors; production, transport, and distribution of gas and electricity, utilities use, for example, SCADA systems to detect current flow and line voltage, to monitor the operation of circuit breakers, etc. These tools can also help in monitoring and controlling pipelines, remotely controlling storage, pumping or refinery sites, or controlling the distribution of electrical energy from various energy sources such as coal, nuclear or gas.

As mentioned above, public transport services can use SCADA systems to regulate the electricity of metros, trams and trolleybuses. In other cases, it is used to automate the signal lights of railway systems, to track and locate buses and trains, control railroad crossing barriers or control traffic flow, detecting, for example, out of order lights. SCADA systems are also used in the sanitation sector. The state and municipalities can use these systems to monitor and control water treatment centers, and installations for collecting and disposing of treated water under the best conditions. Of course, other industries use this software, such as those involved in agriculture and irrigation, pharmaceutical production and telecommunications, among others.

Critical infrastructures are generally spread over a large geographical area, sometimes in deserted places with very few staff on-site, making their security more complex. In addition, the majority of the active elements present in data centers have a life of about five years. The longevity of a CNI is extremely long and can range from ten to twenty years or more (House of Parliament, 2017). Today's systems are lasting longer than in the past, which means that hardware and software are operating beyond their supported lifespan (Cruz et al., 2014). This leads to a cybersecurity strategy that takes into account the fact that existing software or the operating systems used can be out of date. A data acquisition and control system developed to standardize universal access to various monitoring modules within industrial control systems (ICS) (Stouffer et al, 2006) "Industrial Control System (ICS) is an umbrella term that refers to a group of process automation technologies, such as Supervisory Control and Data Acquisition (SCADA) systems and Distributed Control Systems (DCS) (Stouffer et al., 2006), which unfortunately have been subject to a growing number of attacks in recent years" (Maglaras et al., 2018) This architecture, which is an integral part of critical infrastructures, is particularly vulnerable and represents a prime target for hackers because it allows remote technical installations to be controlled. "ICS have unique performance and reliability requirements and often use operating systems, applications and procedures that may be considered unconventional by contemporary IT professionals" (Allan Cook et al., 2017) In addition, and to the great satisfaction of hackers, most communications on these SCADA systems are not encrypted (JunKim, 2017); Current SCADA systems are distributed, networked, and depended on open protocols for the internet, which make them vulnerable to remote cyber terrorism. They are particularly vulnerable to unauthorized access (Maglaras et al., 2018). "These requirements typically follow the priority of availability and integrity, followed by confidentiality and include the management of processes that, if not executed correctly, pose a significant risk to the health and safety of human lives, damage to the environment, as well as serious financial issues such as production losses" (Mitchell and Chen, 2014). In addition, they often require fast responses and interactions between communicating entities, making this equipment very easy target for denial of service (DDoS) attacks: A denial of service or distributed denial of service attack is an attack that aims to make a server inaccessible by sending multiple requests until it is saturated or by exploiting a security hole to cause a failure or a severely degraded operation of the service. This type of attack is extremely complex to block because it is often impossible to differentiate a real request from a request from DDoS. The attack by DDoS very often uses a multitude of zombie PCs infected by backdoors exploited remotely by a pirate and simultaneously attacking a single target. A denial of service attack is also possible with a botnet (Leder, Werner, and Martin, 2009). After having exhausted all the resources of zombie computers and accomplished all their misdeeds, hackers use the botnet system to destroy them.

The botnet is used primarily to send spam. In minutes, they will land on the email addresses of a large number of users on the spammer's list. Spam hits several industries such as finance and health. At the same time, they convey several computer threats such as viruses and phishing. Hackers can collect users' personal data by creating a fake site of their "organization". The information usually collected is the name, the date of birth, the address, the secret code of the credit card, the email address and the password of the user account. By transporting malware via a botnet, the hacker wishes to harm the computer system of the user. The most common malware is worms and viruses. They have the ability to transfer themselves from one IT infrastructure to another via the Internet, e-mails, websites or through the use of USB storage devices, an MP3 player or a camera. Therefore, the botnet can be used as malice to attack or infect a network service and take control of the infrastructure connected to it.

SCADA systems are generally not physically separated from networks. Some companies have a separate network or separate their corporate network. In the following cases, the companies export the same local and wide area network, but the SCADA traffic is in the shared set. This is an easy level to interconnect, and easy to connect to an external transaction. SCADA network equipment can be different from traditional computer systems: They are often installed in places that are difficult to access (for example, in towers, oil rigs and industrial machinery) and have different environmental constraints than standard computer systems (for example, outdoor operation, extreme temperatures, vibrations) or require input voltages and special assemblies. They often use proprietary operating systems that are not enhanced. Their software may not be updated or corrected frequently because of access difficulties, probable downtime or the need to re-certify them. They use proprietary or special protocols.

These different environments create problems such as lack

of authentication and encryption, and weak password storage that allows hackers to access systems. Even though most SCADA networks have some level of defence at their perimeter, including network segmentation and firewall technologies, attackers are still looking for other ways to penetrate the network from the inside, for example, through a backdoor or by triggering actions from within the company to open a communication channel with the outside. Typical attack scenarios are:

1. Using a remote access port usually reserved for a service provider
2. Piracy of a legitimate channel between computer systems and SCADA / ICS systems
3. Convince an internal user to click on a link in an email from a workstation connected to the SCADA / ICS network and the Internet
4. Infecting laptops and / or removable media outside the SCADA / ICS network and then infecting internal systems when they connect to the network to collect data, update the controller / sensors, etc.
5. Exploit security configuration errors or connected devices.

A hacker who has successfully infiltrated a SCADA network would be able to send malicious commands to block or break the device in which he has full control and interfere with the specific critical processes they control, such as opening and closing valves.

Analysing the most active SCADA systems:

- Intouch Wonderware

It is very easy to take in hand, The publisher does not work without a valid license. However, it is Coupled with a very simple and flexible scripting system allowing for the creation of almost all functions. Very effective for very large systems because if the script uses is efficient, it will work without bugs. Intouch has a collective investment fund (CIF) client that allows the user to connect with most commercial PLCs (Programmable Logic Controller: computer-like device, having inputs and outputs, used to automate processes such as controlling machines on an assembly line in a factory). Intouch occupies the largest share of SCADA's software market.

- Vijeo Designer, Schneider

Easy to take in hand, Vijeo designer comes in several versions to program HMI Magelis and graphics terminals. It succeeds Vijeo Citect now obsolete.

- Iconics

The most difficult to handle, complicated enough to understand especially for scripts. However, via the many functions available it can quickly implement small applications. But when the project tends to become more complex, it seems less obvious. It integrates the CIF standard and has a supervision variable limited if it is used without a license.

- Siemens Simatic WinCC

Recently integrated on Siemens' engineering software TIA Portal (Totally Integrated Automation Portal), WinCC can program monitoring panels, Siemens. TIA Portal makes it possible to program PLCs, configure controllers of axes and implement supervision systems all on the same software. TIA Portal is certainly above the competition in terms of ergonomics and simplicity.

- Studio 5000 View Designer Of Rockwell

Allows programming the Rockwell PanelView 5000 Series Supervisory Panels.

- PCView of Arc Informatique

Relatively easy to handle, it has a CIF client and is very popular in the areas of TBM (Technical Building Management) which is a computer system that allows to remotely control the activity of the site and supervise all the equipment installed in it: technical alarms, energy optimization, access management, elevator management ... and CTM (Centralized Technical Management) Which allows remote control of technical installations: alarms, measurements, regulations, modification of parameters (temperature, hours of operation).

• Movicon of Progea

Very easy to learn, variable number limited in evaluation version.

CONCLUSIONS

Cybersecurity is now recognized more than ever before as a vital necessity for the protection of critical infrastructure. Avoiding attacks before they happen requires a combination of knowledge, technology and skills, but also a security-sensitive culture. The importance of security in integrated systems should be emphasized in order to be foresighted by integrating at least two levels of password protection, as well as alarm contacts and signal access failures. This project describes threats, attack scenarios and practical mitigation approaches. Safety is everyone's responsibility, and there are many simple, low-cost steps everyone should take to quickly reduce risks to critical assets. Whether it is regulatory compliance, securing electrical system assets or protecting operational networks and information technology, this paper provides managers with the safety-focused prevention solutions they need. Responses given in this project for cybersecurity provide multi-level protection to critical infrastructure, including the electrical system, transportation, oil, gas, petrochemicals and other operations. This project helps define and develop effective solutions to make the industrial system as secure and reliable as possible. But whatever the preventive measures taken, if they are not focused on resilience, they fall under the imagination, and will not in any case stop a targeted attack against Cis. Business Continuity must be the basis of a better protection policy against Cis, it must describe the strategy of continuity adopted to deal, in order of priority, with risks identified and serialized according to severity of their effects and their plausibility. and the critical infrastructures located on European territory are not spared. The mastery of the cyber threats against an organization, implies a rigorous risk management process based on the methodical identification of the risks surrounding all the internal and external activities of the organization; the assessment of the probability that an event will occur, understanding of how to respond to these events, setting up a strategy to deal with the consequences and monitoring the effectiveness of the organization's risk management approaches and controls. Once these points are identified and highlighted, it helps the process improves decision-making, planning, and prioritization. It also, helps organizations to allocate capital and resources more efficiently to anticipate potential risks thus minimizing any kind of risk including environmental risk consequence of natural disasters.

Since technology has evolved, a lot of things have become smart, bring your own device (BYOD) has become a way of life and the internet of things(IoT) a reality. The risks of an attack also becomes more important but the risk of accidental hazard caused by the environment is as true as that caused by a seated person behind his computer to intentionally cause harm.

Cybersecurity risk assessment assures the company against huge risks that can lead to instability through data piracy, data manipulation or identity theft. Increasingly real risks and the lack of a strategy to identify them and develop a strategy for assessing potential risks that could destabilize a company and undermine its image and reputation would cause harm to the survival of any organization. As a result, solutions to cope with attacks on vital infrastructures have been described in this paper and this is the main objectives of this book. They have been analyzed for a long term result, so that whoever uses them will be able to provide an adequate response to any maltreatment from the attackers.

However, it must be said that the cyber space is not yet in the advantage of the attackers because these new technologies are very expensive and only those attackers who have the financial support from States, can obtain them. On the other hand, States organized themselves in some kind of "organizations" or "agencies" sometimes known sometimes not known to carry out illicit actions against other States by attacking or preparing to attack their "enemy's" critical infrastructures.

Interruptions may not be inevitable, but if they occur, they do not have to slow down the company's activity either be catastrophic. A well-designed Business Continuity Plan, covering IT continuity and user recovery, keeps employees running the business productive. It also helps protect the company from financial losses, a damaged reputation, lower productivity, weaker relationship with customers and partners, weaken the State's deterrent or dissuasion, or loss of lives.

While spending billions of dollars to counter malware and cyber-attacks may be necessary, the diversity, volume, and sophistication of these threats continue to grow. And traditional methods of securing enterprise data and protecting against business interruption have not adequately accommodated the complexity of today's threats. However, any strong critical infrastructure's company needs strong security controls and a global software security perimeter. Disasters do not have to mean latency, and server outages or power outages do not have to put the datacentre at risk. Developing a disaster recovery plan helps ensure the availability and performance of traffic on any network connection and device, not just during disruptions, but at any time. No business is immune to a minor or major disruption, whether it is an event planned as a computer maintenance operation, an office move, an imminent emergency as a hurricane, storm snow, epidemic, or cyberattack, OR a completely unforeseen event without notice, such as an earthquake, tornado, terrorist attack or fire. Even the smallest incident, such as a power outage, transportation delays, or a seasonal flu epidemic, can have a major impact.

Today, resilience must guide action and new regulations and

standards like Network Information Systems (NIS), General Data Protection Regulation (GDPR), require organizations to take action, but if they do not respond to a pragmatic and structured risk-based approach to effectively protect the business and not just respond to a need for compliance, the preparation of the actors may not be sufficient. In other words, and again, the threat, because it is real, must be considered with the utmost seriousness. An attack can negate the trust of users, cause heavy financial losses and damage a company brand image that has taken many years to build. In many cases, the survival of a business and that of States or citizens can depend on it; Thus, the importance of business continuity management.

On the one hand, artificial intelligence can make cyberattacks (denials of service distributed, botnets, ransomware ...) more powerful and effective. The first consequences of the automation of cyberattacks are already being felt, whether they are attacking critical infrastructures or seeking to manipulate public opinion. a distributed malware denial of service attack can turn Internet-connected objects into botnets, remotely-controlled botnets, which can make it difficult to access a large number of Internet sites. Political social bots can also mimic human behavior on social networks to influence users at key political moments. A study of the Computational Propaganda research project at Oxford University showed that one-third of Twitter traffic came from these political bots during the 2016 US presidential election debates.

On the other hand, artificial intelligence technologies can also facilitate and improve the detection and mitigation of cyber-threats. More and more cybersecurity applications are integrating artificial intelligence techniques, including machine learning and predictive analytics, to better identify threats and anomalies. Machine learning allows machines to reproduce and recognize given behaviors from examples. The machines are thus able to process large amounts of data in a short time and to recognize the smallest changes in their environment, differentiating real-time (normal) and threat-threatening behaviors in real-time.

This evolution of cybersecurity will require new skills quite different from those present in current cybersecurity projects and create new trades. Security is increasingly in need of data scientists, specialists in data mining and analysis, as well as experts in data processing in the field of cybersecurity. Above all, an almost "philosophical" change is taking place now: The world is inevitably entering the era of automated cybersecurity, even if the machine, always more efficient, is and will remain in the service of the human. Faced with the resurgence and automation of attacks, it is indeed a machine-versus-machine war that will be witnessed in the coming decades. Big Data and AI will be the first actors in cybersecurity: When artificial intelligence gets involved, it is a vein for IT professionals to use in IT to make security software solutions more "human" in their operation.

RECOMMENDATIONS

This research suggests the application of attenuation techniques whose main objective is to optimize the recovery response. It paves the way for resilience management. it focuses on the calculation and communication capabilities of SCADA-driven CPS to propose new solutions capable of implementing a progressive degradation: the use of alternative (and redundant) copies of the components of the system, associated with the design of different replicas, would mitigate the effects and impact of an attack It may further be to use the reflection through programming, engineering technique allowing a system to adapt to the ability to examine and modify its execution behavior at the time of execution.

This idea about programming could allow a system to react and defend itself against the threats of availability. When malicious activity is detected, the system must change behavior dynamically to activate the correction techniques and ensure the maintenance of its activity.

There are five ways to protect SCADA and ICS networks recommended in this paper:

- Implementation of advanced cyber protection measures. Deploying next-generation firewalls helps protect resources and create micro-segments across the enterprise. With better visibility, attack threats can be reduced.

Secure access to the SCADA area. Implementing processes linking security policies to user identities is recommended to block access to unauthorized users. The deployment of systems such as SSL VPNs (Secure Socket Layered Virtual

Private Network) is perfectly appropriate in this case.

- Eliminate the risk of managing multiple ports. The protection of several ports will have to be provided by one and the same firewall.
- Deployment of a comprehensive protection framework against vulnerabilities. All traffic traversing the SCADA zone is inspected by a complete framework to detect exploits, malware, botnets and other targeted threats.
- Protection of operating systems not supported. The use of a next-generation firewall provides effective protection across the network by detecting attacks that target certain operating systems such as Windows XP and SCADA.

Even in a SCADA environment, organizations benefit from permanent protection despite the removal of support for Windows XP.

Other actions can also be taken, such as:

- Creation of logs and reports of incidents and potential threats.
- The training and use of certain security software.
- The use of aggregation software to centralize logs from different sites to gain global visibility into network usage and security incidents.
- The use of software that facilitates the creation of documents and the regular conduct of cybersecurity audits.
- Lastly, professionals/managers will also need to take a life-cycle approach to threat prevention to control upstream attack vectors, that is, before having to block unknown threats zero-day.

To achieve the required level of protection for industrial and critical networks, security must evolve from simply overlaying technologies to an efficient workflow. An effective security strategy must be able to detect abnormal behavior and block attacks while providing companies with the means to investigate attacks when they occur. The security policy must ensure that any activity is independently logged that is not related to SCADA equipment configuration since it can be hacked by intruders. A repository of the normal behavior of SCADA equipment should define what is allowed, what is prohibited, and what is considered suspicious. Once this is established, the strategy should include automatic notification and prevention of deviations from the repository, to take much more appropriate action against unwanted network exploitation. In addition to establishing a strategy, it is also essential that the entire corporate IT network is secure to protect SCADA equipment.

A key element of multi-layered defense for SCADA equipment should include threat intelligence, to share and gather intelligence on new threats and emerging threats targeting critical infrastructure. This threat intelligence allows companies to defend their network against cyberthreats before they enter, and to better protect SCADA devices and make them less vulnerable to attack.

It is also necessary to use historical data to predict future attacks by using raw data, which will allow using not only current data but also historical data to create statistical baselines to identify normality. Subsequently, it is possible to instantly determine when the data deviates from this standard. Some indicators may not be perceived when presented in real-time, but these indicators maybe even more useful in the long term. This historical data also makes it possible to create predictive models, and statistical models, and offer new opportunities in machine learning. Thus, it is possible to predict future events.

It is also recommended to use Artificial intelligence (AI) tools which will enable States to protect their infrastructures with behavioral detection methods known as attacks prediction techniques which is a preventive policy that consists of attacking before being attacked. This includes, of course, unprecedented cyber-attacks that exploit a loophole that, "no one knew until now" called "zero-day". Most of the time, artificial intelligence will neutralize threats that have existed for more than a year and against which no countermeasures have been deployed.

Good artificial intelligence protection implementation operates from a central point in the network to analyze the flows that pass and fire the alarm when it spots malicious behavior against a target.

AI is an innovative and effective approach to solving problems with computers. Problem-solving is now up to the machine, just describe it for the computer to solve itself. Several methods coexist in this area. One can state several possible solutions and add constraints that will allow the machine to choose the right solution according to these constraints:

- a Sudoku grid for example leaves the choice between several numbers like 1, 4 or 6 to be affixed in the empty boxes but the constraint of not having twice the same number in this grid which already has a 4 and a 6 allows the machine to know that the correct answer is 1. It can also consist of asking the machine to navigate a path between an initial state and a target end-state by choosing the best (the shortest, the fastest, ... the GPS principle). It is said that it runs through a state graph. Finally, problems can be presented to the machine, the solution of which is known and furnished, and pose to it a larger problem composed of several sub-problems of which it knows the solution; its objective will then be to divide the problem into simpler subproblems and thus to solve the problem hat (useful for the grammar of a sentence for example).

- Automatic Language Processing (NLP) or Natural Language is a set of Artificial Intelligence techniques that involve processing computer algorithms for various aspects of human language. It aims to analyze and reproduce artificially spoken language with all its subtleties, input (perception) as output (emission). These are the NLP techniques that tackle very democratized applications such as chatbots, spell check, handwriting interpretation, translations, summaries, search engines, automatic language recognition, document classification.

- The neural network attempts to simulate the synaptic activity of the brain, that is to say, the exchange of information in the sense of "input data - generates - output data". By adding these inter-synaptic spaces in parallel, then by superimposing layers, It aims to generate a "network" of self-regulated weights by the algorithm to which it will simply indicate what is expected in the output according to what has been entered, thus letting the machine make the adjustments between the two.

- The Semantic Web is a domain that currently occupies a key place in the structuring of the Internet and consequently on natural referencing in search engines. It aims to interconnect global web data (W3C standardization) by enabling the machine to understand and contextualize human language. This process considerably improves the search on the internet as the answers are more and more adapted to perfectly meet the expectations of the user. Everything is played out at the level of semantics.

- Expert systems are able to reproduce certain cognitive mechanisms of a human in a very specific field (hence the use of the word "expert"). This software re-transcribes the logic or skills of a person and can effectively perform specific tasks. They thus constitute a saving of time or a decision aid based first on knowledge than on an inference engine (for example a "movement" going from principles to a conclusion). In other words, if a man has a precise and specific know-how in a limited and well-defined area, artificial intelligence will try to reproduce it to facilitate the task of the user (or even do without it).The technique is built on the implementation of rules (basically: "if" ... "then").

- Distributed Artificial Intelligence combines several agents into a single system that is called a multi-agent system. Indeed, it deals with intelligent behaviours that result from the cooperation of several agents, contrary to classical artificial intelligence, in the singular, generally associated with the modeling of the intelligent behavior of a single agent. In this respect, the artificial neural network of deep learning can also be considered a Distributed Artificial Intelligence System. These systems are organized around several intelligent agents whose assembly is made necessary by the objective pursued. Each of these programs is autonomous but they communicate with each other to achieve this goal.

- The most current AI systems with the highest media exposure since 2012 and the overwhelming victory of this technique in the ImageNet Image Recognition Competition mostly work with machine learning, a machine learning technique that allows the machine to evolve without necessarily changing its algorithms.

The computer learns with data (of which it is fed in huge quantities) and can thus perform tasks for which it is not rigidly programmed. This technique is now a big success with Big Data (whose mass of data makes it possible both to "feed the beast" but also to boost the need for recourse to AI helping the human face a volume of which he could no longer come to the end alone). Machine learning, also known as statistical learning, allows a machine to self-correct its analyses based on data captured. It is a simple algorithmic analogy with the human brain: from childhood, it adapts its conclusions according to the data it gathers. For example, when a child first encounters a cat, they say "it's a cat". When he meets a dog for the first time, he says "it's a cat": his parents correct him and say "no, he's a dog" (Heick, 2016). his brain will then automatically distinguish the two animals by what separates them. Then, when another cat arrives, he will assume that he is a cat. From then on, his parents will say "bravo" to him. Then his brain will automatically try to reconcile all the common points between the first 2 cats met (also relying on their differences with the dog) and little by little, the more examples of cats will accumulate, and the more he will recognize cats with a very high percentage of success.

Machine learning has modelled this approach by letting the machine statistically conclude: the machine is provided with input data by telling him "yes" or "no" on its output interpretations while it adjusts itself the weights of the recognition criteria to almost no longer be wrong. Nevertheless, human expertise remains irreplaceable in many ways. First, while machine learning algorithms easily recognize cyberattacks similar to those that have already occurred, they are less effective in identifying new types of attacks. Cyber attackers can also develop adversarial machine learning models to confuse machine learning models that detect threats. Human experience, therefore, remains necessary to correct errors and false positives and to monitor cybercriminal innovations. Secondly, human knowledge and understanding are needed to determine the severity and context of the threat identified by the machine and to choose the most relevant response taking into account the consequences. If human intervention remains necessary, including for ethical reasons, the integration of artificial intelligence techniques allows cybersecurity experts to focus on the most critical tasks - a significant benefit while the cybersecurity industry faces a shortage of talent.

Multi-factor authentication is one of the most effective methods against Phishing, the gateway most used by hackers to get hold of data. Multi-factor identification is a secure connection process in which the user must provide multi distinct identifiers to be recognized and continue to connect in a secure mode. This Multi-level identifier method offers a higher level of protection than that based on a single-factor Authentication(SFA).

In the face of tougher data protection legislation, such as the RGPD(General Data Protection Regulation) in Europe and the UK, or the Cloud Act in the United States, Multi-factor identification is an emergency measure, a first step towards strengthening data security and more generally the user experience online.

The use of machine learning will also help to learn the behavioral patterns of an attack, but Deep Learning goes further by weighting the observations with external knowledge elements. The strength of an AI-based solution that secures the IS with Deep Learning is that protected companies mostly agree to share their information to enrich the algorithms. Thanks to this "collaborative" model, a peculiarity in someone would solve problems for many other clients when it is taken into account everywhere. Conversely, this additional knowledge base makes it possible to train artificial intelligence better so that it knows how to eliminate false positives by itself. Protecting sensitive information may seem rather simple. However, faced with the volume of data to be processed and analyzed to prevent cyberattacks, most companies face a major challenge.

Traditionally, the technologies and tools used to prevent cyberattacks have been more reactive than proactive. They also gave rise to many false alarms. This reduces the efficiency of businesses. This is a distraction from real threats. In addition, these traditional tools do not have the bandwidth required to support large volumes of data.

On the contrary, analytics tools in Big Data offer cybersecurity professionals the ability to analyze different types of data from various sources and react in real-time. These tools not only gather information, but also connect this data, and establish correlations and connections. This makes it possible to increase efficiency and counteract cyberattacks more easily. Big Data can reduce information system vulnerabilities and block cyber-attacks (Janssen and Grady, 2016). Big Data also allows analysts to visualize cyber-attacks by simplifying complex data patterns in the form of data visualizations. The use of machine learning will minimize the human factor in the processing of security alerts: an analyst inattentive or making a mistake may miss a critical element in the detection of an attack. However, human analysis remains crucial in cybersecurity, especially in the remediation and investigation phases. In the case of protection listening to the whole of an environment for example, if machine learning had experimented, it would have made it possible during the WannaCry attack against NHS in the UK to raise an early warning and potentially perform automatic operations to contain the attack during its progression phase. Today's defense best practices are the intelligent integration of on-premise and cloud solutions.

It is essential to set a clear hierarchy for decision-making so that in an emergency, employees do not wonder who is responsible for making a decision The organization should create a business continuity team made up of staff members from across the organization, including executives, IT professionals, site and BC managers, physical security communication, human resources, finance and other services to put in place dedicated support teams for certain tasks, such as emergency response, communication, on-site response and responsiveness.

The company will need to Identify potential business interruptions that could affect any of their organization's sites, such as a power outage, an outbreak, or a fire, to design a plan according to the worst-case scenario, rather than establishing several according to the severity of the accident. This will help to have a manageable number of situations consisting of establishing a list of priorities for the most essential activities, and determining who will carry them out and how the work will be delegated if key personnel are not available. And also, to update the organization's plan each year to reflect changes in application sensitivity and dependency, priorities, risk management, sites, activities, and other factors. Conducting full emergency simulations each year, taking into account crisis communication, safety drills and work environment recovery processes, to evaluate the results of the test and conduct a process of continuous improvement, whether in terms of application availability or staff safety. Creating a crisis communication strategy to develop emergency notification procedures, integrating push and pull systems to communicate quickly to identify all emergency communication stakeholders (Butt, A. et al), including employees, contractors, customers, suppliers, media and management. And to prepare written releases that can be easily updated and transmitted immediately. Training the person in safety procedures to prepare the employees or the users so they know what to do in an emergency and know where to get help, and to consult with local and federal agencies on emergency response training and for further advice on the organization's program to conduct exercises for employees to help staff become familiar with the procedures, including identifying emergency exits.

GLOSSARY

BOYD: the CONCEPT Bring Your Own Device enables businesses to reduce their capital investment costs, this new way of working, however, poses a problem of data security; it also means IT has less control over software and security practices used to access corporate's data through these devices

Resilience: this is basically the ability to bounce back or to decrease the amount of time of disruption when an event happens-the events can be technological or natural disasters.

The term "Internet of Things (IoT): refers to scenarios where network connectivity and computing capacity is extended to everyday objects, sensors, and devices that are not normally considered computers, allowing them to generate, exchange, and consume data with minimal human intervention

The WannaCry Cyberattack: A malicious system that encrypts the data is a virus taking hostage personal data

super-electromagnetic pulsed (EMP): Powerful high-altitude nuclear bombs that can produce super-electromagnetic pulsed (EMP) waves capable of blasting critical electronic infrastructures.

Stuxnet Attacks: is the computer worm that attacks SCADA systems, it can Infect and paralyze a whole system of control-command.

Multi-factor authentication (MFA): is a security system that uses multiple Authentication methods, from different categories of credentials (evidence), to verify identity.

General purpose graphics processing unit (GPGPU): Is password cracking rainbow tables that benefit hackers.

Secure Socket Layered Virtual Private Network (SSL VPNs):

Layer used to to block access to unauthorized users. In this case, Secure access to the SCADA area.

Man-in-the-middle Attack (MIM):

Shadow admin: network accounts that have sensitive privileges and are usually ignored because they are not part of a privileged Active Directory group.

User Behaviour Analytics (UBA): is one of the most promising branches of Artificial Intelligence-based cybersecurity.

Advanced Persistent Threats (APTs): are some of the worst threats today. These tools give to cybercriminals the capability of breaking into the system of their victims to steal sensitive information.

Zero-day: Is an unprecedented cyber-attacks that exploit a loophole that no one knew until it happen

REFERENCES

ANSSI, (2019), EBIOS Risk Manager, what is the ebios risk manager method?, p.4

BundesMinisterium des Innem (2005), Schutz Kritisher Infrastrukturen- Risiko- und Krisenmanagement; Leitfaden fur Unternehmen und Behorden, BMI.

BUTRIMAS, V. (2017). Threat Intelligence Report Cyberattacks Against Ukrainian ICS, Villeurbanne, Sentryo, Research And Lessons Learned Division, NATO Energy Security Center Of Excellence, p.1-2

CERT (2017) Access on 20 Jan 2020, à from : www.us-cert.gov/ncas/alerts/TA17–293A.)

Critical 5 (2014), Forging a Common Understanding for Critical Infrastructure, Shared Narrative 2014, p.2

Cruz, T., Proença, J., Simões, P., Aubigny, M., Ouedraogo, M., Graziano, A., & Maglaras, L. (2014). A distributed IDS for industrial control systems. International Journal of Cyber Warfare and Terrorism (IJCWT), 4(2):1–22, p.22

Ceps Task Force Report, (2010), Protecting Critical Infrastructure In The Eu

Cruz, T., Proença, J., Simões, P., Aubigny, M., Ouedraogo, M., Graziano, A., & Maglaras, L. (2014). A distributed IDS for industrial control systems. International Journal of Cyber Warfare and Terrorism (IJCWT), 4(2):1–22, p.22

Cook, A. (2017). An assessment of the application of it security mechanisms to industrial control systems. International Journal of Internet Technology and Secured Transactions, pp.144,174

CLUSIF, (2019), MEHARI Methodology Overview, Club De La Securite De L'information Français pp..5-7

Directive 2008/114/CE Council Directive on the identification and classification of European critical infrastructure and the assessment of the need to improve its protection.

Denscombe, M. (2007), The Good Research Guide for Small-Scale Social Research Projects, Chapter 9

Denscombe, M. (2010), "The Good Research Guide for Small-Scale Social Research Projects" fourth edition, Butterworth-Heinemann

Dutch A & K Analysis, (1996), Afhankelijkheids- en kwetsbaarheidsanalyse (A&K analysis), Product identity card, https://www.enisa.europa.eu/topics/threat-risk-management/risk-management/current-risk/risk-management-inventory/rm-ra-methods/m_dutch_ak_analysis.html , Access on 20/03/20.

enisa (2018). Analysis of the European R&D priorities in cybersecurity: Strategic priorities in cybersecurity for a safer Europe European Union Agency For Network and Information Security, p.14.

Enisa, (2019), SP800-30 (NIST), Risk Management Guide for Information Technology systems, https://www.enisa.europa.eu/topics/threat-risk-management/risk-management/current-risk/risk-management-inventory/rm-ra-methods/m_sp800_30.html Access on 22/03/2020

Fruhlinger, J. (2017). What is Stuxnet, who created it and how does it work? CSO https://www.csoonline.com/article/3218104/what-is-stuxnet-who-created-it-and-how-does-it-work.html, Access on 16/02/2020

House of Lords House of Commons (2017). Cyber Security Skills and the UK's Critical National Infrastructure: Government Response to the Committee's Second Report of Session 2017–19, p.5

House of Parliament (2017). Cyber Security of UK Infrastructure. the Parliamentary Office of Science and Technology (2017), POSTnote, Number 554, p.1

Hosseini S., Barker K., Ramirez-Marquez J. E. (2016) – A review of definitions and measures of system resilience. Reliability Engineering and System Safety, 145: 47-61.

House of Lords and House of Commons (2018). Joint Committee on the National Security Strategy. Cyber Security of the UK's Critical National Infrastructure. Third Report of Session 2017–19, p.12.

House of Parliament (2017). Cyber Security of UK Infrastructure. the Parliamentary Office of Science and Technology (2017), POSTnote, Number 554, p.1

Hsu, D.F, Marinucci, D. eds. (2012), Advances in cyber security: technology, operations, and experiences. Oxford University Press

Insights (2013a), Bring your own device, Security and risk considerations for your mobile device program, 2013, p.4

Insights (2013b), Bring your own device, Security and risk considerations for your mobile device program, 2013, p.4

Interpol (2018). The protection of critical infrastructures against terrorist attacks: Compendium of good practices, United Of Nations Office of counter-terrorism(UNOCT) and counter-terrorism committee Executive Directorate (CTED), p.19

JunKim, H. (2017).Security and Vulnerability of SCADA Systems over IP-Based Wireless Sensor Networks, Hindawi Publishing Corporation International Journal of Distributed Sensor Networks, Volume 2012, p.2

JunKim, H. (2017). Security and Vulnerability of SCADA Systems over IP-Based Wireless Sensor Networks, Hindawi Publishing Corporation International Journal of Distributed Sensor Networks, Volume 2012, p.2

Jackson, S.L. (2011) "Research Methods and Statistics: A Critical Approach", 4th edition, Cengage Learning, p.17

Kahan J.H., Allen A.C., Georges J.K. (2009) – An operational framework for resilience. Journal of Homeland Security and Emergency Management. 6:1-48.

Leder, F., Werner, T.,. & Martin, P. (2009). Proactive Botnet Countermeasures – An Offensive Approache. Bonn: Institute of Computer Science IV, p.1

Linden, G., Xu, J., Markus, M.,Morefield, D., Lokuciejewski, P., Engels, R., Olbrich, N., Dufur, C., Diaz, L.J., Heure, J., Larson, U., Khare, S., Thiruvenkatachari, B., Menna, A., Cooper, C., & Smith, L. (2019). Reinventing Cybersecurity with Artificial Intelligence: The new frontier in digital security, Capgemini research institute,2019 p.12-14.

Leder, F., Werner, T.,. & Martin, P. (2009). Proactive Botnet Countermeasures – An Offensive Approache. Bonn: Institute of Computer Science IV, p.1

McAfee, (2011), McAfee's 2010 report, "In the Crossfire: Critical Infrastructure in the Age of Cyberwar.", p. 6

Mike M. Khayat, (2002), Wireless Local Area Network (WLAN) Advantages vs. Disadvantages, INNS 690, Professional Seminar, 2002, pp.5,6

MOULINOS, K. (2019), Enisa, Incentives and barriers for the cyber insurance market in Europe, Enisa, pp.7-11

Michael Phox (2017). Computational Security And The Economics Of Password Hacking, pp.3-9

Mitchell, R. and Chen, I. (2014). A survey of intrusion detection techniques for cyber-physical systems. ACM Computing Surveys (CSUR), p.55

Mitchell, R. and Chen, I. (2014). A survey of intrusion detection techniques for cyber-physical systems. ACM Computing Surveys (CSUR), p.55

Maglaras, L., Kim, K., Janicke, H., & Ferrag, M.A. (2018). Cyber security of critical infrastructures. ICT Express, SCADA systems Security, p.2

Maret, S. (2016). On Their Own Terms: A Lexicon with an Emphasis on Information-Related Terms Produced by the U.S. Federal Government, 6th ed., revised 2016, p.1

Muller, R. (2014). Advanced Persistent Threats: Defending from the Inside Out, CA Technologies, Security Management, white paper, p.4

Ministry of the Interior and Kingdom Relations. National Coordination Centre (2004), Critical Infrastructure Protection in the Netherlands. The Dutch approach on Critical Infrastructure Protection, The Netherlands, http://www.minbzk.nl/

Minister of the interior http://www.niscc.gov.uk/niscc/aboutCNI-en.html.

Ministry of interior and kingdom relation , National Coordination Centre (2004) Critical Infrastructur Protection in the Netherlands. The Dutch approach on CNI, The Netherlands, http://www.minbzk.nl/

NHS Southern Health. (2018), Bring Your Own Device (BYOD) Policy, ICT Security Policy, version 2, p.4

OSCE, (2014), OSCE REPORT 2013, p.28 & pp.93-94

OSCE, (2014), Annual Report 2013, p.34

Pry, P.V., (2017). Nuclear Emp Attack Scenarios And Combined-Arms Cyber Warfare, Report To The Commission To Assess The Threat To The United States From Electromagnetic Pulse (Emp) Attack, p.1

Pry, P.V., (2017a). Nuclear Emp Attack Scenarios And Combined-Arms Cyber Warfare, Report To The Commission To Assess The Threat To The United States From Electromagnetic Pulse (Emp) Attack, p.1

Pry, P.V., (2017b). Nuclear Emp Attack Scenarios And Combined-Arms Cyber Warfare, Report To The Commission To Assess The Threat To The United States From Electromagnetic Pulse (Emp) Attack, p.5

Pillai, B., Mehta, V., & Patel, N. (2012). Development of Supervisory Control and Data Acquisition system for Laboratory Based Mini Thermal Power Plant using LabVIEW, International Journal of Emerging Technology and Advanced Engineering Website: www.ijetae.com ISSN 2250-2459, Volume 2, Issue 5, p.449

Pursiainen C., Rod B. (2016) – Report of criteria for evaluating resilience. IMPROVER Report D2.2

Peter, M., Bruenjes, R., Cohen, M., Freeman, J., Graf, R., Kilani,

M. O'Leary, C., Pashley, C., Ryan, J., Shannon, G., Walters, G., & Wills, T. (2018) Cyber Resilience and Response. US Department Of Homeland Security, Public-private Analytic exchange program, p.5

Recommendations of the National Institute of Standards and Technology, Special Publication 800-82 INITIAL PUBLIC DRAFT 2006, p.2-1

Rebecca Slayton, (2015), Measuring Risk: Computer Security Metrics, Automation, and Learning, Access on 20/03/2020 https://www.computer.org/csdl/magazine/an/2015/02/man2015020032/13rRUxYrbOi

Roger A. Grimes, (2011), Massive 'Lurid' APT attack targets dozens of government agencies, INFOWORLD TECH WATCH, site: https://www.infoworld.com/article/2620437/massive--lurid--apt-attack-targets-dozens-of-government-agencies.html, Access on 23/03/2020

Stouffer, K., Falco, J., & Kent, K. (2006). NIST, Guide to Supervisory Control and Data Acquisition (SCADA) and Industrial Control Systems Security,

Site CGDN http://www.sgdn.gouv.fr/, Access on 18/03/220

Symantec (2011a). Advanced Persistent Threats: A Symantec Perspective, Preparing the Right Defense for the New Threat Landscape, white paper: cutting through the hype, p.4

Symantec (2011b) Advanced Persistent Threats: A Symantec Perspective, Preparing the Right Defense for the New Threat Landscape, white paper: cutting through the hype, p.2

Sheila Frankel, Bernard Eydt, Les Owens, Karen Kent, (2006), Guide to IEEE 802.11i: Establishing Robust Security Networks (Draft), Recommendations of the National Institute of Standards and Technology, NIST Special Publication 800-97, 2006, p.11.

Stouffer, K., Falco, J., & Kent, K. (2006). NIST, Guide to Supervisory Control and Data Acquisition (SCADA) and Industrial Control Systems Security, Recommendations of the National Institute of Standards and Technology, Special Publication 800-82 INITIAL PUBLIC DRAFT 2006, p.2-1

The IP chapter, (2020), Economic And Trade Agreement Between The United States Of America And The People's Republic Of China Fact Sheet, Intellectual Property, pp. 1-5

The register, (2012), By John Leyden 29 Aug 2012 at 09:18,https://www.theregister.co.uk/2012/08/29/saudi_aramco_malware_attack_analysis/

UN Council resolution 2341 (2017), Protection of Critical infrastructure against terrorist acts adopted Feb 2017

Wang, Y., Liu, J., Yang, C., & Zhou, L. (2018) Access Control Attacks on PLC Vulnerabilities, Scientific Research Publishing, Journal of Computer and Communications, pp.311-313.

Webb, W. (2002). Cyber Defense Initiative: FTP Security and the WU-FTP File Globbing Heap Corruption Vulnerability, SANS Institute 2000 – 2002, GCIH Practical Assignment Version 2.0, pp.10-11

Yazar, Z. (2002), A qualitative risk analysis and management tool – CRAMM, (GSEC, Version 1.3), p.5

Info entrepreneurs (2019) Crisis management and business continuity planning. Available at https://www.infoentrepreneurs.org/en/guides/crisis-management-and-business-continuity-planning/ (Accessed: 12 April 2019).

Advisera Expert Solutions Ltd (2016) Clause-by-clause explanation of ISO 22301, white paper, 27001 Academy ISO 27001 and ISO 22301 Online consultation center, p.4.

World Health Organization (2007) Risk reduction and emergency preparedness, WHO six-year strategy for the health sector and community capacity development, p.9.

Whitcher, R. (2009) BCI 'BS 25999 – a framework for resilience and success', BSI Management Systems, Raising Standards Worldwide, June, p.15.

Janes,T. and Kerr H. (2019) Horizon Scan Report, Business continuity institute, p.6.

Department For Transport. (2011) Business Continuity Management Policy', Dft BCM Policy, P.8.

Cisco. (2015) Enterprise Mobility: Securing a Productive and

Competitive Future, Cisco white paper, January, pp.4-5.

Google. (2017) The Google Android Security Team's Classifications for Potentially Harmful Applications, Google, Inc. Android Security, February, pp.1-4.

NHS. (2016) NHS England Emergency Preparedness, Resilience and Response (EPRR), Business Continuity Management Toolkit, February, p.7.

Butt, A. et al. (2016) Project change stakeholder communication, International Journal of Project Management 34 (2016) 1579–1595, p.4

Zhang, Y. Li, X. Zhang, S. Zhen, Y.(2012), Wireless sensor network in smart grid: Applications and issue. In Information and Communication Technologies (WICT), 2012 World Congress on (pp. 1204-1208). IEEE.

BIBLIOGRAPHY

Allix, K., Jerome, Q., Tegawen,´ F., Bissyand,´E., Klein, J., State, R., and Le Traon, Y. (2014). A Forensic Analysis of Android Malware How is Malware Written and How it Could be Detected? IEEE 38th Annual International Computers, Software and Applications Conference, Interdisciplinary Centre for Security, Reliability and Trust, University of Luxembourg. [Accessed 12 May 2019]

Executive Office of the President of the United States (2016). PREPARING FOR THE FUTURE OF ARTIFICIAL INTELLIGENCE, Executive Office of the President National Science and Technology Council Committee on Technology, Washington. [Accessed 20 May 2019)

HMG Security Policy Framework (2018). Minimum Cyber Security Standard, version 1.0, https://www.25062018_minimum_cyber_security_standard_gov.uk_3
[Accessed 12 May 2019]

La Polla, M., Martinelli, F., and Sgandurra, D. (2013). A Survey on Security for Mobile Devices, 446 IEEE COMMUNICATIONS SURVEYS & TUTORIALS, VOL. 15, NO. 1, [Accessed 21 May 2019]

Yardley, T. (2008). SCADA: issues, vulnerabilities, and future directions, vol. 33 No. 6, pp1-6. Available at : https://www.usenix.org/system/files/login/articles/258-yardley.pdf [Accessed 17 April 2019]

Interpol (2018). The protection of critical infrastructures against terrorist attacks: Compendium of good practices, United Of Nations Office of counter-terrorism(UNOCT) and counter-terrorism committee Executive Directorate (CTED),

p.19
ECHO 4 (2002). Disaster Preparedness and Prevention (DPP): State of play and strategic orientations for EC policy Working Paper, EUROPEAN COMMISSION HUMANITARIAN AID OFFICE, Commission européenne, B-1049 Bruxelles / Europese Commissie, B-1049 Brussel, pp. 5-6

HM Government survey (2015). 2015 Information Security Breaches Survey. Technical report pwC and Info security Europe, p.11

Knapp, E. and Langill, J. (2014). Industrial Network Security: Securing critical infrastructure networks for smart grid, SCADA, and other Industrial Control Systems. Syngress, p.3

Rubio-Hernan, J., Sahay, R., De Cicco, L., & Garcia-Alfaro, J. (2018). Cyber-physical architecture assisted by programmable networking. Internet Technology Letters, p.6.

Domović, R. (2017). Cyber-attacks as a threat to critical infrastructure. Zagreb University of Applied Sciences Vrbik 8, Zagreb, Croatia, p.2

Segovia, M., Cavalli, A.R., Cuppens, N., & Garcia-Alfaro, J. (2018). A Study on Mitigation Techniques for SCADA-driven Cyber-Physical Systems. 11th International Symposium on Foundations & Practice of Security (FPS 2018), Springer LNCS, Montreal, Canada, p.12

Laddaga, R., Robertson, P., Shrobe, H., & Cerys, D., (2019a). Deriving Cyber-security Requirements for Cyber Physical Systems, Vanderbilt University and DOLL Labs, Inc. and 3MIT Nashville, TN and Lexington, MA and Cambridge, MA, p.2.

Maroti, M., Kecskes, T., Kereskenyi, R., Broll, B., Volgyesi, P., Juracz, L., Levendovszky, T., & Ledeczi, A. (2014). Next generation (meta) Modeling: Web- and cloud-based collaborative tool infrastructure. Multi-Paradigm Modeling,1237: pp.41 – 60.

Symantec (2011). Advanced Persistent Threats: A Symantec Perspective, Preparing the Right Defense for the New Threat Landscape, white paper: cutting through the hype, p.4

Muller, R. (2014). Advanced Persistent Threats: Defending

from the Inside Out, CA Technologies, Security Management, white paper, p.4

Palo Alto Networks (2019). Industrial Control Systems, Santa Clara, Security Reference Blueprint for Industrial Control Systems | White Paper, pp. 3-7

World Meteorological Organization (2006). Guide on use of FTP and FTP servers at WWW centres, p.7

ipswitch (2017), Ransomware Vulnerabilities and File Transfer. P.5

Check Point (2018). Protecting Industrial Control Systems And Scada Networks, Check Point software technology ltd, white paper, p.1

Bon, G., & van Loon, S. (2006). Password cracking in the field: operating systems and database management systems, Amsterdam, Research Report System and Network Engineering University of Amsterdam, pp. 13-15.

Hecht, A., And Lazarovitz, L. (2018). Sneak Your Way To Cloud Persistence - Shadow Admins Are Here To Stay, San Francisco RSA Conference2018, session ID: HT-RO4,pp. 22-29

Pry, P.V., (2017). Nuclear Emp Attack Scenarios And Combined-Arms Cyber Warfare, Report To The Commission To Assess The Threat To The United States From Electromagnetic Pulse (Emp) Attack, p.1

Linden, G., Xu, J., Markus, M.,Morefield, D., Lokuciejewski, P., Engels, R., Olbrich, N., Dufur, C., Diaz, L.J., Heure, J., Larson, U., Khare, S., Thiruvenkatachari, B., Menna, A., Cooper, C., & Smith, L. (2019). Reinventing Cybersecurity with Artificial Intelligence: The new frontier in digital security, Capgemini research institute,2019 p.12-14.

Michael Phox (2017). Computational Security And The Economics Of Password Hacking, pp.3-9

CTED Trend report (2017). Physical Protection Of Critical Infrastructure Against Terrorist Attacks, United nations security council Counter-Terrorism Committee Executive Directorate, p.1

Appendix A: Project Plan

Table 13: Breakdown of results Apendix (From Own Work, Data 2020-UK)

Task	Time Spend/ month
Preparing Documents for the survey	2
Survey	8
Structuring method	2
Research	4
Analysing the results	1
Taking notes	3
Writing the report	1

Printed in Great Britain
by Amazon